LOTUS
Prayer Book

LOTUS
Prayer Book

*"More things are wrought by
prayer than this world dreams of."*

Alfred, Lord Tennyson

INTEGRAL YOGA® PUBLICATIONS, YOGAVILLE, VIRGINIA

Compilation © 1986 by
Satchidananda Ashram – Yogaville.
Previously unpublished material by
Sri Swami Satchidananda © 1986
by Satchidananda Ashram – Yogaville.
2nd Printing 1995

Library of Congress Cataloging in Publication Data
LOTUS prayer book.
    Includes index.
    1. Prayers.   2. Prayer.   I. Integral Yoga Publications (Firm).
BL560.L67   294.5'43   86-10384
ISBN 0-932040-33-0
Integral Yoga® Publications
Satchidananda Ashram - Yogaville
Route 1, Box 1720
Buckingham, Virginia 23921

Printed in the United States of America

*With deepest gratitude and reverence
this Prayer Book is lovingly dedicated to*

*Sri Swami Satchidanandaji Maharaj,
on the occasion of the Dedication of
the Light Of Truth Universal Shrine,
20 July 1986.*

*May these sacred prayers from the various faiths be a
testimony to Sri Swamiji's essential teaching that
"Truth is One, Paths are Many."*

LOTUS PRAYER

O Lord, the Light of Lights,
You are the Indweller of the entire Universe.
You are the Light of Awareness.
You are the Light of our Consciousness.
You are the One who enlightens everything and
　　　everybody.
You are the One who makes the sun shine,
　　　the moon shine, who makes the stars shine, who
　　　makes the fire burn.
Kindly lead us to that Light of Wisdom and remove
　　　the darkness of ignorance; enlighten our hearts.
Help us experience that Light within and without.
Help us see the same Light, the same Spirit dwelling
　　　everywhere in everything or, to be more
　　　accurate, as everything.
Help us to understand You and You alone through
　　　all these various forms and names, through all
　　　these different approaches and ways of worship.
Help us recognize the central unity.
Help us realize we are Your image, Your children,
　　　no matter what the differences are.
Let us behold Your Spirit running through all.
Give us the strength and courage and capacity to
　　　experience that Peace and Joy within and share
　　　the same with everyone.

Help us to get away from these selfish temptations
    with which we are creating all the differences, all
    the fights, and all the wars.
We have suffered enough due to our ignorance.
Please guide us to know our brothers and sisters
    and to know we are all parts of Your family.
Enlighten our paths, O Light of Lights, Lord
    of Lords. Help us, guide us.

Sri Swami Satchidananda

CONTENTS

PREFACE

The idea for this prayer book was conceived by the Reverend Sri Swami Satchidananda, as a way to show the essential unity of all faiths through devotional and sacred writings. It was brought to fruition through the loving service and prayers of the many members of the Integral Yoga family, and especially those at the San Francisco Integral Yoga Institute.

The cover design was provided by Rev. Arjuna Jyothi, and the book design and production were overseen by Robert Cooney. The type was set by John Greenslade and Michael Sykes at Archetype West.

Publication was made possible through the generous donations of many people. Special thanks to:

Kiki Brubeck
Lydia Deems & Bill Prothero
Saraswati & Janardhana Epstein
Jai & Shakti Fink
Nischala & Manu Godfirnon
Padma & Prasant Hansma
Meenakshi Honig
Ted Johnson
Irmgard Knitt
Krishnprema & Bob Mouw
Badrinath Rodrigues

Tara & Rishi Schweig
Dawn Summers
Janaki Tompkins
Radha & Ram Vignola

It was truly a privilege and blessing to compile these prayers, to be immersed in the thoughts and feelings of so many great souls, and to see more clearly that we are all One in Spirit, ever seeking, finding, and delighting in the Divine. May that irresistible call of the Divine kindle universal Love and perfect Joy in the hearts of all!

Swami Karunananda Ma

ACKNOWLEDGMENTS

Our thanks to the following for the use of material:

Selections on pages 110, 128, 146, and 167 from *The Shasta Abbey Book of Ceremonies* (Mt. Shasta: Shasta Abbey Press, 1979), ©P.T.N.H. Jiyu-Kennett, by permission of the publisher.

Native American selections on pages 38 (second selection), 55, 161, 171, and 198 from *The Sacred Pipe: Black Elk's Account of the Seven Rites of the Oglala Sioux,* recorded and ed. by Joseph Epes Brown, © 1953 by University of Oklahoma Press, by permission of the publisher.

The John G. Neihardt Trust for selection on page 71 from *Black Elk Speaks* by John G. Neihardt.

Selections by Lao Tsu on pages 13, 27, 45, 46, 109, 127, 145, 166, and 180 from the *Tao Te Ching,* by Lao Tsu, trans. by Gia-fu Feng and Jane English, © 1972 by Gia-fu Feng and Jane English, reprinted by permission of Alfred A. Knopf, Inc.

Selections by Lao Tsu on pages 26, 64, and 192 from *The Tao,* an edition by Tolbert McCarroll (New York: Crossroad Publishing Co., 1982), by permission of Tolbert McCarroll.

Selection from the *Mundaka Upanishad* on page 20 from *The Vedic Experience, Mantramanjari,* © 1977 by Raimundo Panikkar, by permission of Raimundo Panikkar.

American Israel Publishing Co. for children's prayers on pages 178, 179, and 182 from *My Shalom, My Peace,* ed. by Jacob Zim and Uriel Ofek, trans. by Dov Vardi.

All Sikh selections from *Peace Lagoon,* comp. and trans. by Sardarni Premka Kaur, by permission of Arcline Publications.

Writings of Paramahansa Yogananda by permission of Self-Realization Fellowship.

INTRODUCTION

Background

A very beautiful and unique temple is the inspiration for this prayer book. It is called LOTUS — the Light Of Truth Universal Shrine.

It is built in the shape of a lotus flower. The lotus has long been a symbol for the unfolding of spirituality. It rises from the mud and lifts its face to the sun, revealing its magnificent beauty for all to enjoy. Though it lives in the water, it is not affected by it, just as spirit pervades matter without being affected.

Within the Shrine there are twelve altars, one in each petal of the lotus. There is an altar for each of the ten major faiths, as well as one for all other known faiths, and one for all that are still unknown. In the center is a light that rises to the top of the dome, where it splits into twelve rays and then descends to illuminate each of the altars. Thus, a very powerful and inspiring statement is made about the essential unity of all faiths — that all have the same Universal Light as their source.

If everyone realized this great truth — that we are one family, children of the one God — the world would be transformed into a heaven. Honoring and enjoying our differences, we could come together to live in peace and harmony.

With this vision in mind, the Reverend Sri Swami Satchidananda, a world-renowned spiritual leader and Yoga Master, began this project. For many years he led Yoga Ecumenical Services, in which clergy from different faiths gathered to worship around a central light, sharing from their own traditions. Witnessing the heartfelt peace and joy experienced by the participants, he was inspired to create a permanent place where all could come to realize this oneness.

The LOTUS has been built in the heart of Satchidananda Ashram – Yogaville, a spiritual center in Buckingham, Virginia. People from all backgrounds have come there to lead dedicated lives in the spirit of universal brotherhood. Together, they are helping to create a model village where all can live healthy, peaceful, useful lives.

LOTUS Prayer Book

This book is a ray from the LOTUS light, an expression of the great truth that LOTUS represents. Its purpose is to show that the yearning and aspiration for the Divine, as well as the ultimate transcendental experience, are universal.

Prayer comes from the innermost heart, and in the heart, we are all truly one. Through prayer we can see our unity and the one divine Light as the source of all.

Prayer can take many forms. There are prayers of petition, intercession, thanksgiving, praise, blessing, and affirmation. In petition, the grace of the Supreme is implored to fulfill some need or request; in intercession, such requests are made in behalf of another. In prayers of thanksgiving, gratitude to the Almighty is voiced; in praise, the Divine is glorified. In blessing, the power of God is invoked to bless, protect, and guide oneself and others. In prayers of affirmation, expression is given to such heartfelt concerns as one's faith, one's relationship to the Divine, and the spiritual nature and order of the Universe.

People from all faiths and cultures throughout history have envisioned and called to God in remarkably similar ways; the same themes recur in their prayers. A number of these themes have been selected and illustrated with prayers from the ten major religions represented at LOTUS, as well as from the lesser known faiths.

It is our sincere hope that the prayers in this book will be a source of comfort, guidance, and light, and will also serve as messengers of unity and brotherhood.

May all be blessed to experience the supreme Peace and Joy within and to share it with one and all!

GUIDE FOR USING THIS BOOK

The following symbols are used to indicate the religions from which the prayers come:

ॐ HINDUISM   ☪ ISLAM

✡ JUDAISM   ☬ SIKHISM

⛩ SHINTO   🔺 AFRICAN

☯ TAOISM   ✳ NATIVE AMERICAN

☸ BUDDHISM   ☺ OTHER KNOWN RELIGIONS

✝ CHRISTIANITY

For more detailed information about the sources of the prayers, please refer to the *Index of Sources* at the end of the book.

4

THE POWER
OF PRAYER

I asked God for strength, that I might achieve,
I was made weak, that I might learn humbly to
    obey.
I asked for health, that I might do greater things,
I was given infirmity, that I might do better things.
I asked for riches, that I might be happy,
I was given poverty, that I might be wise.
I asked for power, that I might have the praise of
    men,
I was given weakness, that I might feel the need
    of God.
I asked for all things, that I might enjoy life,
I was given life, that I might enjoy all things.
I got nothing that I asked for — but everything
    I had hoped for.
Almost despite myself, my unspoken prayers were
    answered.
I am, among all men, most richly blessed.

American Confederate Soldier

PRAYER

by Sri Swami Satchidananda

Prayers are powerful, good thoughts. A sincere prayer that comes from a faithful heart can perform miracles. Have that faith. Many, many things can happen by prayer. A great thinker once said: "More things are wrought by prayer than this world dreams of."

God is really everywhere, not in a particular form, but as an omnipresent awareness or power. God is consciousness itself. By your concentrated sincere prayer, you are tuning your mental radio to receive that power. By tuning the radio, you are not creating music. It is already there; your tuning merely attracts the radio waves. When you tune your mind to the proper wavelength, you will receive God's grace and experience cosmic consciousness.

If your prayer is not answered, don't blame God for that. You may pray for ten years and get nothing, whereas somebody else might pray for one minute and get everything. This depends on the quality of your prayer, how honestly and sincerely you pray. The sincerity in seeking comes only when you know that you have a limited capacity. It's only when you say, "I can't do it anymore, please help me," that the help comes. You then link yourself with an unlimited capacity. Sometimes God acts like a hard-hearted person. He waits until you really give up and the last bit of your egoism is renounced.

If you want God to come in, make room. When you become aware of your smallness, it opens your mind. All of nature is ready to give to you. You need not go and praise the sun to get light. Just open the window and the sunlight comes in. As long as you don't put up a barrier, you get light. In the same way, God is ready to help you. Don't allow your pride to get between you and God's help.

In prayer you may use a lot of words, but that is not the real prayer. The real prayer comes after you finish speaking. The words simply prepare your mind. You finish the prayer and you just become still. In deep prayer, you forget everything. You forget your body, mind, and personality. You lose yourself. Momentarily, you become God and you can do all that God does. When you come down to the normal level again, you may say, "God gave me that," but God didn't give it to you. You received it because you had His capacity momentarily.

Deep prayer always comes from the heart. It's not the head that prays, it's the heart. When you sing or pray to God from your very heart, you don't have to worry if you hit the right note. God understands our innermost prayer. Many children communicate with their mothers in this way, by a sound no one else understands. Sometimes when the baby cries, only the mother understands, because theirs is a special language.

A true devotee is the one who has complete faith in God. He trusts in God as a baby trusts in the mother. He accepts everything in life as God's will. He never questions God. And in his prayer he just expresses his trust and faith. He doesn't even ask God for anything. He knows that God will give him everything that he needs, even without asking, and He will not give him anything that is not good for him, even if he asks.

In the *Bhagavad Gita* four kinds of devotees are mentioned. The first asks God to remove his suffering. The second requests material things. The third prays for liberation. But the fourth does not ask for anything. He just enjoys praying and praising God. This is the highest form of prayer.

The great Saint Ramalingam prayed to the Lord: "You are feeding me; I am fed. You are making me sleep; I am sleeping. You are showing me; I am seeing. You are making me happy; I am happy. And not only me — the entire universe is like that. You are the One behind every movement, every experience." If you want to have a prayer, pray to God to help you to always remember this Truth: that you are His child and He is taking care of you every minute.

PRAYER

by Sri Swami Sivananda

Prayer is the effort of man to commune with the Lord. It is a mighty spiritual force. It is as real as the force of gravity or attraction.

Prayer does not demand high intelligence or eloquence. God wants your heart when you pray. Even a few words from a humble, pure soul, though illiterate, will appeal to the Lord more than the eloquent, flowing words of an orator or a lecturer.

When you pray, you are in tune with the Infinite. You link yourself with the inexhaustible cosmic storehouse of power and thus draw power, energy, light, and strength from Him.

Attune your heart with the Lord by doing fervent and sincere prayer daily. Lay bare your heart to Him. Do not keep any secrets. Talk to Him like a child. Be humble and simple. Implore Him with a contrite heart to forgive your sins. Beseech Him to bestow His Grace. Do not depend upon human help. Rely on God and God alone. You will get everything. You will get His vision.

If you pray regularly, you life will be gradually changed and moulded. Prayer must become habitual. You will feel as if you cannot live without prayer, if prayer becomes a habit in you.

Prayer produces tremendous influence on the body and mind. It purifies the mind, invigorates and sharpens the intellect, and generates beneficial and healthy spiritual currents. It develops the power of understanding. All incurable diseases are cured through sincere true prayer.

There are no problems that cannot be dissolved by prayer; no suffering that cannot be allayed by prayer; no difficulties that cannot be surmounted by prayer; and no evil that cannot be overcome by prayer. Prayer is communion with God. Prayer is the miracle by which God's Power flows into human veins. Therefore, kneel down and pray. Remove now the darkness of ignorance through the divine light of prayer!

THE POWER OF PRAYER

The prayer of a pure heart never goes unanswered.
— *Mahatma Gandhi*

The Lord is nigh unto all them that call upon Him, to all that call upon Him in truth.   — *a Psalm of David*

I believe that all things come to pass according to our prayers; there is no such a thing as failure of prayer by the True-Self.   — *Kurozumi Munetada*

The Tao of heaven does not speak, and yet is answered; it does not ask, yet is supplied with all its needs.   — *Lao Tsu*

He who with a steady heart raises his voice and without ceasing prays shall be freed from his sins.
— *Buddhist scriptures*

In very truth I tell you, if you ask the Father for anything in my name, He will give it to you.

— Jesus Christ

Everything which you ask of Him, He gives to you; and if you would reckon the favours of God, you could not count them! *— The Holy Koran*

Use your tongue to recite His praises day and night, For this is the gift of God Himself. *— Guru Arjun*

If Pagong pray, God the Great One is brought to the country. *— Dinka of Sudan*

If one of mine prays to me properly, I shall be with him. *— Omaha Indians*

Pray to God and fill your heart with His pleasure, so that you may be sure to be filled with goodness by Him. *— Zend-Avesta*

LIGHT

Oh Great Effulgence of Grace
Who transported me over the great boundless sea
called birth and rid me of my misery! . . .

Oh Great Effulgence of Grace
Who are the beginning of everything
and are beginningless in Yourself
and Who do not take note of caste, creed, and
    religion! . . .

Oh Great Effulgence of Grace
biggest of the big and smallest of the small,
and rarest of the rare! . . .

Oh Great Effulgence of Grace
Who, abiding in my mind,
create therein an immeasurable enlightenment
that it may spread all over the world! . . .

Oh Great Effulgence of Grace
Whose great glory soars majestically,
You bade me:
"Do experience all the mishaps
which beset the creatures of this earth,
that you may remove them;
and do so remove them and rejoice,
and gain the happy state of the Pure Truth."

St. Ramalingam

Oh gracious Light
in the sun,
in the beauty of the sun,
in its form and formlessness,
in its tongues of flame,
in its flame within the flame,
in the sheaves of solar rays,
in the focused light of the sun,
in its radiating light!
Oh Light Who becoming one
with the core of the light
and the light of the light,
dance therein most auspiciously!
Oh my Sire, Oh my King
Who, on that night in the past,
came and bestowed on me
the Light of Grace!
Oh Wise One! Oh Ambrosia!
Oh Lover! Oh Bliss! Oh Father!
Oh Gracious One!
Oh Delight of my life
which has sought You!
Oh Unique One! Oh Pure One!
Oh my Friend!
Oh Treasure of Pure Blissful True Path,
Oh my Spouse, Nataraajaa,
the Great Effulgence of Grace!

St. Ramalingam

ॐ

Oh Lord Who, filling the sky and the earth,
transcends them in the form
of a dazzling Effulgence!
Oh Lord Who, beyond concept of the human
    mind,
has a form without limits!
When You, the Lord with an eye on the forehead,
arrived at where I was,
and beckoned me with Your gracious glance,
I of evil karma
did not in the least know
how to worship
Your beyond-reach-of-thought lovely feet
or how to praise Your great glory.
As grass, shrub, worm, tree,
as full many a kind of beast, bird, snake,
as stone, man, goblin, demons,
as mighty giants, ascetics, devas,
in the prevalent world of animate and inanimate
    forms—
O my noble Lord, I have been born
in every kind of birth, and am wearied!
O Reality! Your golden feet I saw this day
and deliverance from birth gained!

Maanikkavaachakar

O blazing Light! awaken my heart, awaken my soul,
ignite my darkness, tear the veil of silence, and fill my
temple with Thy glory.

Paramahansa Yogananda

In the highest golden sheath is the Godhead,
Unsullied, indivisible;
Pure is it, the Light of lights.
He who knows the Self knows it.
Neither the sun nor moon nor stars shine there.
Neither lightning nor fire finds there a place.
With the radiance of that Light alone all things
    shine.
That radiance illumines all this world.

Mundaka Upanishad

The Lord is my light and my salvation; whom shall
  I fear?
The Lord is the stronghold of my life; of whom shall
  I be afraid?
When evil-doers came upon me to eat up my flesh,
Even mine adversaries and my foes, they stumbled
  and fell.
Though a host should encamp against me,
My heart shall not fear;
Though war should rise up against me,
Even then will I be confident.

One thing have I asked of the Lord, that will I seek
  after:
That I may dwell in the house of the Lord all the
  days of my life,
To behold the graciousness of the Lord, and to visit
  early in His temple.
For he concealeth me in His pavilion in the day
  of evil;
He hideth me in the covert of His tent;
He lifteth me up upon a rock.
And now shall my head be lifted up above mine
  enemies round about me;
And I will offer in His tabernacle sacrifices with
  trumpet-sound;
I will sing, yea, I will sing praises unto the Lord.

from a Psalm of David

O Living God, we thank Thee that Thou hast not left us to grope after Thee in the dark; that Thy law has been a lamp unto our feet, and a light unto our path. In this harvest season, when Thy people had gathered in their crops, Thy law did enjoin upon them to leave their homes and make their abode in frail booths. Thus didst Thou remind them of the transient nature of earthly possessions, of the insecurity of a life stayed on prosperity without faith in Thee.

Vouchsafe unto us, too, O Father, an understanding of this truth, so that no arrogance may tarnish the joy of success, no self-exaltation debase the love of achievement. Teach us to be humble. Keep far from us the pride of possession and the despair of want. In poverty save us, O God, from bitterness; in abundance rescue us from self-indulgence. Incline our hearts unto Thee and keep us from covetousness. Kindle within us a passion for a better world. Enlarge our sympathies, make us eager to ease the sorrow and distress of others and thus learn to know the joy of service. Lift up our eyes that, like our fathers, we too may see through the leafy booth, the light of sun and star, so that our souls may soar to Thee.

Prayer for the Feast of Tabernacles

The Light of Divine Amaterasu shines forever
Even now as in the Age Divine.

O the Joy to think that the Heaven-Shining-
      Goddess and Man
Both are One, un-separated, and at once Divine.

When the Heart of the Shining-Goddess and my
      Heart
Are One, this is indeed Eternal-Life.

Kurozumi Munetada

⛩

Abiding in Her magnificent shrine,
She shines Her protecting rays far
To the lands of the four corners,
Her radiant light bringing peace
Everywhere under the heavens.

Ise Shrine

⛩

Like unto the Sun's bright light, eternal,
Shining from above the skies—
Bless, Oh Goddess, with thy care supernal,
Generations yet to rise!

Emperor Gonara

Essence of the Supreme One,
Spirit of the obscure mystery,
You who produce all beings
    and who can purify all,
      before invoking you I sprinkle myself
      and place myself in this pure place.
By order of the Sovereign Lord
    the seven celestial torches were lit.
They send their rays on this earth,
    lighting and protecting all living beings.
Assistants and ministers of the right and left,
    brilliant and redoubtable intellects;
O chief of the heavenly army
    and you five thunder-bearers;
Leave for a moment the golden palace;
    come to this dusty world
    to deliver us from dangers and evils,
    to protect and prolong our lives.
Extend to us your power,
    extinguish that which is bad and impure,
    bless all those who live,
    give repose to the dead.
May those who disobey you perish.
May they who obey you prosper.
The seven celestial torches shine,
    spreading their light on our persons.

May this protecting light
    cause us to live always!
With respect we offer incense.
With reverence we express our devotion.

Taoist prayer

See the small and develop clear vision.
Practice yielding and develop strength.
Use the outer light to return to the inner light,
And save yourself from harm.

Lao Tsu

A good walker leaves no tracks;
A good speaker makes no slips;
A good reckoner needs no tally.
A good door needs no lock,
Yet no one can open it.
Good binding requires no knots,
Yet no one can loosen it.

Therefore the sage takes care of all men
And abandons no one.
He takes care of all things
And abandons nothing.

This is called "following the light."

Lao Tsu

O Amitabha, light without equal . . .
O Amitabha, infinite splendor . . .
    so pure and so calm . . .
    so sweet and so consoling . . .
How we desire to be reborn with thee!
Thou whose power is without limits . . .
Thou toward whom the beings
    of all the worlds turn,
How beautiful is thy kingdom,
    where the breeze sows flowers
    under the feet of the blessed . . .
How we desire to be reborn with thee!
How beautiful is thy kingdom,
    where the finest music resounds,
    where the most precious perfumes rise,
    where all beings are saints . . .
How we desire to be reborn with thee!
Foolishly, during numberless existences,
    we have renewed the karma
    which binds us to the earth.
Oh! guard us henceforth, sweet light,
    that we lose no more the wisdom of the heart!
We exalt thy knowledge and thy works;
    we desire that all may go to thee,
    that no obstacle may prevent any being from
    being reborn in peace and happiness with you!

In Praise of Amitabha

The radiance of Amida Buddha's Light of Truth
    surpasses all,
So He is called the Buddha of Pure Light;
Those who are embraced in the Light
Are cleansed from the dirt of karma and attain
    emancipation.

However far His light illumines, love penetrates,
The joy of faith is attained,
So we are told.
Take refuge in the Great One who gives comfort.

Shinran Shonin

✝

Dear Jesus, help us to spread your fragrance
    everywhere we go.
Flood our souls with your spirit and life.
Penetrate and possess our whole being so utterly
    that our lives may only be a radiance of yours.
Shine through us, and be so in us,
    that every soul we come in contact with
    may feel your presence in our soul.
Let them look up and see no longer us
    but only Jesus!
Stay with us, and then we shall begin to shine
    as you shine; so to shine as to be a light to others;
    the light, O Jesus, will be all from you,
    none of it will be ours;
    it will be you, shining on others through us.
Let us thus praise you in the way you love best
    by shining on those around us.
Let us preach you without preaching, not by words
    but by our example, by the catching force,
    the sympathetic influence of what we do,
    the evident fullness of the love
    our hearts bear to you. Amen.

Cardinal Newman

✝

O merciful Jesus, enlighten me with the brightness of thine inward light, and take away all darkness from the habitation of my heart.

Repress thou my many wandering thoughts, and break into pieces those temptations which so violently assault me. . . .

Send out thy light and thy truth that they may shine upon the earth, for until thou enlighten me I am but as earth without form and void.

Thomas à Kempis

✝

O what intoxication of light,
O what movements of fire!
O what swirlings of the flame in me,
    miserable one that I am,
    coming from You and Your glory! . . .
I thank You that, even when I was sitting
    in darkness, You revealed Yourself to me,
    You enlightened me,
You granted me to see the light of Your
    countenance that is unbearable to all.
I remained seated in the middle of the darkness,
    I know, but while I was there
    surrounded by darkness,
You appeared as light, illuminating me completely
    from Your total light.
And I became light in the night, I who was found
    in the midst of darkness.

St. Symeon

Allah is the Light of the heavens and the earth. His light is like a niche in which there is a lamp. The lamp is in a glass. The glass is, as it were, a shining star. This lamp is kindled from a blessed tree, an olive, neither of the East nor of the West, whose oil would almost glow forth of itself, though no fire touched it. Light upon light, Allah guideth unto His light whom He will.

The Holy Koran

O God, give me light in my heart and light in my tomb, and light in my hearing and light in my sight, and light in my feeling and light in all my body, and light before me and light behind me, and light on my right hand and light on my left, and light above me and light beneath me. O Lord, increase light within me, and give me light, and illuminate me.

Abu Talib

ੴ

The Lord put His light in this body, and so it came
    into the world.
Yes, it came into the world when the Lord
    illumined the mind with His light.
The Lord Himself is the Father and the Mother,
    who created creatures so that they might see the
    world.
When one realizes the reality, by the Grace of the
    Guru,
One comes to know that this world is a mere show.
Sayeth Nanak: Thus the Lord created the universe,
Putting His light in every being.

Guru Amar Das

Thy Light is abiding in the soul,
Unextinguished day and night.
Thy arms reach everywhere, and Thou art King
of kings.

Thou art King of kings, and Sun of suns.
Thou art God of gods, and great is Thy praise. . . .

Thou art the Master of the earth and sky.
Thy deeds are boundless.
Thou art supreme in forgiveness.
Thou art brave and dazzling.

Inextinguishable light,
Endless forgiveness,
Inconceivable form,
Thy possessions are unlimited. . . .

I bow to the Sun of suns, I bow to the Moon
of moons.
I bow to the King of kings, I bow to the Lord of
Indras.
I bow to Thy form of darkness, I bow to Thy form
of Light.
I bow to the Highest of the high.
I bow to the Seed of seeds.

Guru Gobind Singh

O Sun,

As you rise in the east through God's leadership,

Wash away all the evils I have thought of throughout
the night.

Bless me, so that my enemies will not kill me and
my family;

Guide me through hard work.

O God, give me mercy upon our children who are
suffering.

Bring riches today as the sun rises;

Bring all fortunes to me today.

Luyia from Kenya

From the great rock I see it, the Daybreak Star, the
    sign of the dawning;
Above the mountain it rises and my heart dances.
Now the light comes, the light that makes me one
    with all life.
Like the tinamou I am, who sings in the dawn,
    who is humble with love,
Who walks in the circle of the greater love and
    the greater power.
Let me be like a ray of light, like a flower blazing
    with light,
Like the waterfall laughing with light, like the great
    tree also,
Mighty in its roots that split the rocks, mighty in its
    head that reaches the sky,
And its leaves catch the light and sing with the wind
    a song of the circle.

Let my life be like the rainbow, whose colors teach
    us unity;
Let me follow always the great circle, the roundness
    of power,
One with the moon and the sun, and the ripple of
    waters,
Following the sacred way of honor, a guide and
    protector to the weak,
A rock of strength in my word that shall say no evil,
    no lie nor deception.

Let me be like the otter, so loyal to his mate he will
    die for her,
So strong to his children they obey him as the
    shadows obey the sun;
And let me remember always the Great One, the
    Lord of the Dawning,
Whose Voice whispers to me in the breeze, whose
    words come to me out of all the circles of life,
    and whose command is like the thunder:
"Be kind, be kind, be brave, be brave, be pure,
    be pure,
Be humble as the earth, and be as radiant as the
    sunlight."

Guaymi

The Sun, the Light of the world,
I hear Him coming.
I see His face as He comes.
He makes the beings on earth happy,
And they rejoice.
O Wakan-Tanka, I offer to You this world of Light.

Kablaya of the Oglala Sioux

I believe Thee to be the best being of all, the source of light for the world. Everyone shall choose Thee as the source of light, O most beneficent spirit, Divine Being. For Thou, O Lord, shall be unto us as the everlasting light.

Zend-Avesta

I think over again my small adventures,
My fears,
Those small ones that seemed so big,
For all the vital things
I had to get and to reach.
And yet there is only one great thing,
The only thing,
To live to see the great day that dawns
And the light that fills the world.

Innuit

O Samas, thy light penetrates to the uttermost
    depths, to the unknown depths of the sea.
O Samas, thou clingest to all;
Thy shield covers all lands. . . .
No god in all the universe is so powerful.
At thy rising, all the gods of the land unite;
Thy splendorous light showers down upon the
    earth.
From every corner, at the sound of any tongue,
Thou knowest their thoughts and guidest their steps.
In thy name all men rejoice, O Samas,
For the universe ardently desires thy light.

Mesopotamia

CREATOR

ॐ

Beloved Lord, humble prostrations.

May I realize that You are my creator and You have a
purpose in my existence here in this world. Often my
little ego comes in the way and makes me think that I
am the doer and that I should get all the fruit of Your
actions through this instrument. Please do something, say turn a switch or something, so that my
ego — or is it not Your ego given to me to be called
mine — will never bother me.

My Lord, I am just a puppet in Thy hands.

Sri Swami Satchidananda

Praised be Thou, O Lord our God, Ruler of the world, who in Thy mercy makest light to shine over the earth and all its inhabitants, and renewest daily the work of creation. How manifold are Thy works, O Lord! In wisdom hast Thou made them all. The heavens declare Thy Glory. The earth reveals Thy creative power. Thou formest light and darkness, ordainest good out of evil, bringest harmony into nature and peace to the hearts of all.

Sabbath prayer

Since Amaterasu-O-Mi-Kami is the Great-Goddess who gives birth to everything in Heaven and Earth, indeed to All-Creation without exception, and accomplishes everything which is done in the Universe, I pray only that I may entrust everything absolutely to the Honourable-Sun-Disc.

Kurozumi Munetada

The Tao begot one.
One begot two.
Two begot three.
And three begot the ten thousand things.

The ten thousand things carry yin and embrace˙
    yang.
They achieve harmony by combining these forces.

Lao Tsu

All things arise from Tao.
They are nourished by Virtue.
They are formed from matter.
They are shaped by environment.
Thus the ten thousand things all respect Tao and
    honor Virtue.
Respect of Tao and honor of Virtue are not
    demanded,
But they are in the nature of things.

Therefore all things arise from Tao.
By Virtue they are nourished,
Developed, cared for,
Sheltered, comforted,
Grown, and protected.
Creating without claiming,
Doing without taking credit,
Guiding without interfering,
This is Primal Virtue.

Lao Tsu

✝

O most high, almighty, good Lord God, to Thee belong praise, glory, honor, and all blessing!

Praised be my Lord God with all His creatures, and specially our brother the sun, who brings us the day and who brings us the light; fair is he and shines with a very great splendor: O Lord. he signifies to us Thee!

Praised be my Lord for our sister the moon, and for the stars, which He has set clear and lovely in heaven.

Praised be my Lord for our brother the wind, and for the air and cloud, calms and all weather by which Thou upholdest life in all creatures.

Praised be my Lord for our sister water, who is very serviceable unto us and humble and precious and clean.

Praised be my Lord for our brother fire, through whom Thou givest us light in the darkness; and he is bright and pleasant and very mighty and strong.

Praised be my Lord for our mother the earth, which doth sustain us and keep us, and bringeth forth divers fruits and flowers of many colors, and grass.

Praised be my Lord for all those who pardon one another for His love's sake, and who endure weakness and tribulation; blessed are they who peaceably shall endure, for Thou. O most Highest, shalt give them a crown.

Praised be my Lord for our sister, the death of the body, from which no man escapeth. Woe to him who dieth in mortal sin! Blessed are they who are found walking by Thy most holy will, for the second death shall have no power to do them harm.

Praise ye and bless the Lord, and give thanks unto Him and serve Him with great humility.

St. Francis of Assisi

✝

O how scarce the number of souls who wish to let the divine Creator work within them, who suffer in order not to suffer, and die in order not to die! How few are the souls that wish to deny themselves, to cleanse the heart of its longings, desires, satisfactions, of its self-love and judgment! How few who wish to follow the path of negation and the inner light! Who wish to obscure themselves, dying to their senses and to themselves! How few wish to vow, purify, and lay themselves bare, that God might dress them and fill them with perfection!

Molinos

✝

O Thou eternal One! whose presence bright
    All space doth occupy, all motion guide;
Unchanged through time's all-devastating flight;
    Thou only God! there is no God beside!
Being above all beings! Mighty one!
      Whom none can comprehend and none
      explore,
Who fill'st existence with thyself alone;
      Embracing all, supporting, ruling o'er;
      Being whom we call God, and know no
      more! . . .

Thou from primeval nothingness didst call
    First chaos, then existence; Lord, on Thee
Eternity had its foundation; all
      Sprang forth from Thee — of light, joy,
      harmony
Sole origin; all life, all beauty, Thine.
      Thy word created all, and doth create;
Thy splendor fills all space with rays divine.
      Thou art, and wert, and shalt be, glorious,
      great,
      Life-giving, life-sustaining Potentate! . . .

Creator, yes! thy wisdom and thy word
    Created me! Thou Source of life and good!
Thou Spirit of my spirit, and my Lord!
    Thy light, thy love, in their bright plenitude,
Filled me with an immortal soul, to spring
    O'er the abyss of death, and bade it wear
The garments of eternal day, and wing
    Its heavenly flight beyond this little sphere,
Even to its source — to Thee — its Author, there.

Gavriil Romanavich Derzhavin

☪

One Thou exaltest, and givest him dominion,
Another Thou castest as food to the fishes;
One Thou enrichest with treasure, like Karun,
Another Thou feedest with the bread of affliction:
Nor is that a proof of Thy love, nor this of Thy
    hatred;
For Thou, the Creator of the World, knowest what
    is fit;
Thou assignest to each man his high or low estate:
And how shall I describe Thee? THOU ART
    WHAT THOU ART!

Ferdusi

Thou art the Primal Being, the most Excellent
  Creator.
There is none other as great as Thee.
From age to age, Thou art ever and ever One;
Thou art always the same: Immovable Creator.
Whatever is pleasing to Thee, that comes to pass.
Whatever is done is done by Thee.
Thou it was Who created all things,
And having designed them Thou shalt also destroy
  them.
Slave Nanak sings the praises of that Lord, Who is
  All-Knowing.

Guru Ram Das

Let us lift our voices in prayer,
Offering up an ox to the Creator.
May this ox be permitted to grow old,
That we may gain good health.
Let us lift our voices in prayer,
Offering up an ox to the Creator.
The Creator of the sky gives us peace,
Gives us food.

Dinka from Sudan

Great Spirit!
Piler up of the rocks into towering mountains!
When thou stampest on the stone,
The dust rises and fills the land.
Hardness of the precipice;
Waters of the pool that turn
Into misty rain when stirred.
Vessel overflowing with oil!
Father of Runji,
Who seweth the heavens like cloth:
Let him knit together that which is below.
Caller forth of the branching trees:
Thou bringest forth the shoots
That they stand erect.
Thou hast filled the land with mankind,
The dust rises on high, oh Lord!
Wonderful One, thou livest
In the midst of the sheltering rocks,
Thou givest of rain to mankind:
We pray to thee,
Hear us, Lord!
Show mercy when we beseech thee, Lord.
Thou art on high with the spirits of the great.
Thou raisest the grass-covered hills
Above the earth and createst the rivers,
Gracious One.

Shona from Zimbabwe

Grandfather, Wakan-Tanka, You have always been and always shall be. You have created everything — there is nothing which does not belong to You. You have brought the red people to this island, and You have given us knowledge that we may know all things. We know that it is Your light which comes with the dawn, and we know that it is the Morning Star who gives us wisdom. You have given us the power to know the four Beings of the universe and to know that these four are really One. We see always the sacred heavens, and we know what they are and what they represent. This day will be a great day, and all that moves upon the earth and in the universe will rejoice.

Moves Walking of the Oglala Sioux

Creator of the world,
Maker of all men;
Lord of all Lords,
My eyes fail me
For longing to see thee,
For the sole desire to know thee.
Might I behold thee,
Might I know thee,
Might I consider thee.
Might I understand thee.
Oh, look down upon me,
For thou knowest me.
The sun — the moon —
The day — the night —
Spring — winter —
Are not ordained in vain
By thee, O Vira-cocha!
They all travel
To the assigned place;
They all arrive
At their destined ends,
Withersoever thou pleasest.
Thy royal scepter
Thou holdest.
Oh, hear me,
Oh, choose me;
Let it not be
That I should tire,
That I should die.

PARENT

My Lord!
In this world below, when a father beats an unruly son, the mother runs to his protection, throws her arms around her son and clasps him to her bosom;

And when a mother beats an unruly son, the father holds his son by his hand and shields him from the anger of the mother.

But to me, the remorseful Sinner, Thou Who art ever dancing in mercy in the hearts of all lives, with Thy ineffable Form of Energy, infinite and variegated — Thou art the protecting Father, and Thou art the protecting Mother, too.

So, I beseech Thee Who art both Father and Mother to me, to cease beating me, who can no longer bear the anguish of it, and give me refuge in the effulgent shade of Thy Holy Feet.

St. Ramalingam

Alas, I do not know either Thy Mantra or Yantra (mystical word-symbol or diagram), or songs of praise to Thee, or how to welcome Thee or meditate upon Thee; neither do I know words of praise to Thee, nor Thy Mudra (mystical hand gesture), nor how to inform Thee of my distress; but this much I know, O Mother, that to take refuge in Thee is to destroy all my miseries. . . .

O Mother, Thou hast many worthy sons on earth, but amongst them I am most insignificant, yet it does not befit Thee, O Shivā, to forsake me, for a bad son may sometimes be born, but there is never a bad mother. . . .

That Pashupati, the Lord of creatures who is besmeared with the ashes of the funeral pyre, who has swallowed poison and has the quarters of the world for His garments, who has matted hair and is garlanded with the King of serpents, and who holds a skull as a begging bowl in His hands, is dubbed the Lord of the universe, because of His marriage with Thee, O Mother Bhavani.

I have no desire for liberation, nor for wealth and knowledge; neither am I desirous of happiness, O Moon-faced One, but this much I beg of Thee, O Mother, that my life may be spent reciting Thy names. . . .

O Mother of the universe, there is nothing to be wondered at if Thou shouldst be full of compassion for me, for a mother does not forsake her son even if he has innumerable faults.

There is not such a sinner like me, neither such a destroyer of sins as Thou. O Mahadevi, having known all this, do as Thou thinkest fit.

Sri Shankaracharya

O God, who art the strength of all that trust in Thee, my soul is filled with gratitude for the numberless blessings Thou bestowest on me. With a father's tender care Thou rememberest me every day and every hour.

Teach me, O Lord, to obey Thy will, to be content with what, in Thy wisdom, Thou hast allotted to me, and to share Thy gifts with those who need my help. Guide me, O Father, with Thy good counsel, and hold in Thy keeping the lives of those dear to me. May Thy presence dwell within my home; may peace and happiness abide in it, and love unite all who live under its shadow. And when, in Thy wisdom, Thou sendest trials and sorrows, grant me strength to bear them patiently, and courage to trust in Thy help. Guard Thou my going out and my coming in, now and evermore. Amen.

Sabbath prayer

Please let me acknowledge the immortal life and
   eternal activity of the Universe.
Let me acknowledge that the Universe is the
   presence of Kami.
Let me acknowledge that I am the beloved child
   of the Parent Kami.
Let me acknowledge that I am living amidst the
   infinite benevolence of the Universe.
Let me acknowledge that the Universe is my
   eternal home.
Let me acknowledge that there is a broad highway
   of truth along which I should travel.
Let me acknowledge the everlasting mediation of
   Ikigami Konko Daijin.

Konko Sect

All things under heaven had a common
　　beginning, and that beginning could be
　　considered the Mother of all things.
When you know the Mother, you will also know
　　the children.
Know the children, yet hold fast to the Mother,
　　and to the end of your days you will be free
　　from danger.

Lao Tsu

Even as a mother at the risk of her life
　　would watch over her own, her only child,
So let us with boundless mind and goodwill
　　survey the whole world.

Sutta-Nipata

✝

O garment of the sun, bride of light, born of the
    Father, filled with divine spirit, show us the
    splendor of justice, thou who changed the
    beauty of Eve.
Thou walkest with the moon, shinest brighter than
    any star, hearest the songs of angels, Mother of
    light, Heaven's gate, now and forever.
On thy head is a crown of twelve stars in
    wondrous order; O Virgin, give us the Son as
    the stars give us rays.
O rose of the thorny plant, thou makest the lily bloom.
As clear as the dawn, splendorous, advance sweetly
    to us, come to us from the race of Jesse, from
    Aaron's rod, covered with flowers and leaves,
    O fruit of the almond tree.
Gleaming star of the sea, port of refuge, not all
    the storms of death can hurl us into the inferno.
    Give aid to the shipwrecked on the seas of the
    world; intercede for them if they confide in thee. . . .
Through thy compassion, keep us from falling into
    sin through the idleness of our ways and of our
    nature.
In all the vast arch of Heaven there is none more
    worthy of praise than she, nor any similar to
    her, the Virgin Mary, bride of God, most
    humble Mother.

In Praise of the Virgin Mary

✝

Lord, I know not what I ought to ask of Thee; Thou only knowest what I need. Thou lovest me better than I know how to love myself. O Father, give to Thy child that which he himself knows not how to ask.

I simply present myself before Thee; I open my heart to Thee. Behold my needs which I know not myself; see, and do according to Thy tender mercy. Smite, or heal; depress me, or raise me up. I adore all Thy purposes without knowing them; I am silent, I offer myself in sacrifice, I yield myself to Thee.

I would have no other desire than to accomplish Thy will. Teach me to pray; pray Thyself in me.

François Fénelon

✝

Lord, sanctify to us alike the light and shadow of life, alike its fruitions and failures, and may it bring us nothing of joy or woe that shall not be a ministry of grace to our spirits. Unless Thou keep us, O Lord, our life will lose its secret of power and its soul of hope; hide us in the sanctuary of Thy love. Visit in Thy mercy all who are in dire plight of faith by reason of bitter sorrow, all for whom the sun is veiled by the pale cast of fear or foreboding.

Minister to us, our Father; help us to know Thee, not as in the word of a prophet, but by what we are and have within us of Thine eternal life.

The Reverend Joseph Fort Newton

Just as the mother, who gives birth to her son,
Feeds him and keeps him always in her vision;
Indoors or outdoors, she sees that he has food,
And sometimes caresses him:
So the True Guru watches over the disciple who has
    love and affection for his God.
O Lord, we are all Thy foolish children.
Hail, all hail, unto the True Guru, who has made
    me wise by revealing God's instructions.

The white clad flamingo flies through the sky,
While she all the time keeps her young ones in her
    thoughts;
They have been left behind, but she ever remembers
    them in her heart.
Just so, the True Guru keeps the disciple pressed to
    his heart,
By instilling in him the love of the Lord.

Guru Ram Das

O My Father, Great Elder,
I have no words to thank you,
But with your deep wisdom
I am sure that you can see
How I value your glorious gifts.
O My Father, when I look upon your greatness,
I am confounded with awe.
O Great Elder,
Ruler of all things earthly and heavenly,
I am your warrior,
Ready to act in accordance with your will.

Kikuyu from Kenya

O Mawu Sodza, Mother of men, Mother of beasts. If thou givest to man, thou givest truly. If thou deniest to man, thou deniest truly. In thy greatness, I am great and agree to thy will.

Ewe from Dahomey, Ghana, and Togo

Father, a needy one before Thee stands. I am he.

Omaha

Grandfather, Great Spirit, lean close to the earth that you may hear the voice I send. You towards where the sun goes down, behold me; Thunder Beings, behold me! You where the White Giant lives in power, behold me! You where the sun shines continually, whence come the day-break star and the day, behold me! You where the summer lives, behold me! You in the depths of the heavens, an eagle of power, behold! And you, Mother Earth, the only Mother, you who have shown mercy to your children!

Hear me, four quarters of the world — a relative I am! Give me the strength to walk the soft earth, a relative to all that is! Give me the eyes to see and the strength to understand, that I may be like you. With your power only can I face the winds.

Great Spirit, Great Spirit, my Grandfather, all over the earth the faces of living things are all alike. With tenderness have these come up out of the ground. Look upon these faces of children without number and with children in their arms, that they may face the winds and walk the good road to the day of quiet.

This is my prayer; hear me! The voice I have sent is weak, yet with earnestness I have sent it. Hear me!

Black Elk of the Oglala Sioux

Hail to our Mother who makes the yellow flowers
    to bloom, who scatters the seeds of the maguey
    as she comes from the Land Divine!

Hail to our Mother who casts forth white flowers in
    abundance!

Hail to our Mother who shines in the thorn bush
    as a bright butterfly!

Ho! She is our Mother — the woman god of the
    earth. In the desert she feeds the wild beasts.

Thus, you see her ever abundant gifts to all flesh.

And as you see the goddess of the earth give to the
    beasts, so also does she give to the green herbs
    and the fishes.

Hail to our Mother who casts forth yellow flowers
    to the sun from the Land Divine.

Mexican

Holy is God the Father of all, who is before the
first beginning;

Holy is God, whose purpose is accomplished by his
several Powers;

Holy is God, who wills to be known, and is known
by them that are his own.

Holy art Thou, who by Thy word hast constructed
all that is;

Holy art Thou, whose brightness nature has not
darkened;

Holy art Thou, of whom all nature is an image.

Holy art Thou, who art stronger than all
domination;

Holy art Thou, who art greater than all pre-
eminence;

Holy art Thou, who surpassest all praises.

Accept pure offerings of speech from a soul and
heart uplifted to thee, Thou of whom no words
can tell, no tongue can speak, whom silence only
can declare.

I pray that I may never fall away from that
knowledge of Thee which matches with our
being; grant Thou this my prayer.

And put power into me, so that having obtained
this boon, I may enlighten those of my race who
are in ignorance, my brothers and Thy sons.

Wherefore I believe and bear witness that I enter
into Life and Light.

Blessed art Thou, Father; Thy Man seeks to share
Thy holiness, even as Thou hast given him all
authority.

Graeco-Roman

LOVE

ॐ

Dear One, come and bestow Thy vision on me.
Without Thee, O Love, I cannot be.
As the lotus without the water, as the night without
    the moon,
So do I — Thy maid, feel without Thee.
Troubled and distracted, I move about night and
    day long,
While the pangs of separation gnaw at my heart.
The days pass without hunger, and the nights go
    without sleep.
When words do not come out of the lips,
How can I complain without speech?
Except Ye, O Lord, what other hope can I cherish?
Come, soothe this burning heart.
Come, be kind and meet me, O my Master.
Mira, Thy maid of ages,
In supplication falls at Thy feet.

Mirabai

Unbearable to me
Is my separation
From the Lord, my Beloved.
I am pining in anguish.
O Thou, my life, my light, my love!
This separation from Thee
Breaks my heart.
What shall I do?
Where shall I go
To see my Beloved?
My eyes rain tears.
Every second is prolonged to an eternity.
Come, my darling, come!
In Thy mercy, come!

Sri Swami Sivananda

ॐ

O my divine Master, my love aspires after Thee more intensely than ever; let me be Thy living Love in the world and nothing but that! May all egoism, all limitations, all obscurity disappear; may my consciousness be identified with Thy Consciousness so that Thou alone mayest be the will acting through this fragile and transient instrument.

Oh my sweet Master, with what an ardour my love aspires for Thee.

Grant that I may be only Thy Divine Love and that in everything this Love may awaken powerful and victorious.

Let me be like an immense mantle of love enveloping the whole earth, penetrating all hearts, murmuring to every ear Thy divine message of hope and peace.

O my divine Master, with what an ardour I aspire for Thee! Break these chains of darkness and error; dispel this ignorance, liberate, liberate me, make me see Thy light.

The Mother, Sri Aurobindo Ashram

ॐ

In the center of my heart I have a mystic throne for Thee. The candles of my joys are dimly lighted in the hope of Thy coming. They will burn brighter when Thou appearest. Whether Thou comest or not, I will wait for Thee until my tears melt away all material grossness.

To please Thee my love-perfumed tears will wash Thy feet of silence. The altar of my soul will be kept empty until Thou comest.

I will talk not; I will ask naught of Thee. I will realize that Thou knowest the pangs of my heart while I wait for Thee.

Thou dost know that I am praying; Thou dost know that I love no other. Yet whether Thou dost come to me or not, I will wait for Thee, though it be for eternity.

Paramahansa Yogananda

Thy lovingkindness, O Lord, is in the heavens;
Thy faithfulness reacheth unto the skies.
Thy righteousness is like the mighty mountains;
Thy judgments are like the great deep;
Man and beast Thou preservest, O Lord.
How precious is Thy lovingkindness, O God!
And the children of men take refuge in the shadow
    of Thy wings.
They are abundantly satisfied with the fatness of
    Thy house;
And Thou makest them drink of the river of Thy
    pleasures.
For with Thee is the fountain of life;
In Thy light do we see light.

from a Psalm of David

✝

I beseech Thee, O Lord, that the fiery and sweet strength of Thy love may absorb my soul from all things that are under heaven, that I may die for love of Thy love as Thou didst deign to die for love of my love.

St. Francis of Assisi

✝

Where have You hidden,
Beloved, and left me moaning?
You fled like the stag
After wounding me;
I went out calling You, and You were gone. . . .

Why, since You wounded
This heart, don't You heal it?
And why, since You stole it from me,
Do You leave it so,
And fail to carry off what You have stolen?

Extinguish these miseries,
Since no one else can stamp them out;
And may my eyes behold You,
Because You are their light,
And I would open them to You alone.

St. John of the Cross

✝

Let the whole creation praise Thee, O Thou Lord of the world! Oh, that a voice might go forth over all the earth, proclaiming Thy faithfulness to those who love Thee! All things fail; but Thou, Lord of all, never failest! They who love Thee, oh, how little they have to suffer! Oh, how gently, how tenderly, how sweetly Thou, O my Lord, dealest with them! Oh, that no one had ever been occupied with any other love than Thine! It seems as if Thou didst subject those who love Thee to a severe trial: but it is in order that they may learn, in the depths of that trial, the depths of Thy love. O my God, oh, that I had understanding and learning, and a new language, in order to magnify Thy works, according to the knowledge of them which my soul possesses! Everything fails me, O my Lord; but if Thou wilt not abandon me, I will never fail Thee. Let all the learned rise up against me, let the whole creation persecute me, let the evil spirits torment me — but do Thou, O Lord, fail me not; for I know by experience now the blessedness of that deliverance which Thou dost effect for those who trust only in Thee.

St. Teresa of Avila

☪

O Lord, grant us to love Thee; grant that we may love those that love Thee; grant that we may do the deeds that win Thy love. Make the love of Thee to be dearer to us than ourselves, than our families, than wealth, and even than cool water.

Muhammad

☪

I have loved Thee with two loves,
A selfish love and a love that is worthy of Thee.
As for the love which is selfish,
Therein I occupy myself with Thee, to the
    exclusion of all others.
But in the love which is worthy of Thee,
Thou dost raise the veil that I may see Thee.
Yet is the praise not mine in this or that,
But the praise is to Thee in both that and this.

Rabi'a al-'Adawiyya

Just as a man with a great thirst longs for
    refreshing water,
So does my soul have a deep longing for the sight
    of the Lord.
Like an arrow, love of the Lord has pierced my
    heart.
Only the Beloved Lord knows my pain and what
    suffering is mine.
I will accept as my companion and my brother,
Any man who can tell me a tale of my Beloved
    Lord.
So, come all my brothers and friends,
Let us join together in praise of the Lord,
And follow the instructions of the most patient
    True Guru.
O Lord, Slave Nanak asks that you but fill his one
    desire:
That I may behold Thee, and my body and soul find
    peace!

Guru Ram Das

Give us, O God, the vision which can see Thy love in the world in spite of human failure. Give us the faith, the trust, the goodness in spite of our ignorance and weakness.

Give us the knowledge that we may continue to pray with understanding hearts, and show us what each of us can do to set forth the coming of the day of universal Peace. Amen.

First Prayer from Space, from Apollo 8

BEAUTY

ॐ

O Presence of ineffable beauty, O thought of supreme redemption, sovereign power of salvation, with what joy all my being feels Thee living in itself, sole principle of its life and of all life, marvelous constructor of all thought, all will, all consciousness. Upon this world of illusion, this sombre nightmare, Thou hast bestowed Thy divine reality, and each atom of matter contains something of Thy absolute.

Thou art, Thou livest, Thou art radiant and reignest.

The Mother, Sri Aurobindo Ashram

In my middle years I knew something of Tao
And finally settled on south mountain.
When the spirit moves, I wander alone
Amid beauties that only I know . . .
I will walk till the waters end,
Then sit and watch the rising clouds,
And perchance meet an old man of the woods,
And talk and laugh and never return.

Wang Wei

✝

Late have I loved Thee, O Beauty so ancient and so new; late have I loved Thee! For behold Thou wert within me, and I outside; and I sought Thee outside and in my unloveliness fell upon those lovely things that Thou hast made. Thou wert with me and I was not with Thee. I was kept from Thee by those things, yet had they not been in Thee, they would not have been at all. Thou didst call and cry to me and break open my deafness; and Thou didst send forth Thy beams and shine upon me and chase away my blindness; thou didst breathe fragrance upon me, and I drew in my breath and do now pant for Thee; I tasted Thee, and now hunger and thirst for Thee; Thou didst touch me, and I have burned for Thy peace.

St. Augustine

☪

O my Lord, if I worship Thee from fear of Hell, burn me in Hell, and if I worship Thee from hope of Paradise, exclude me thence, but if I worship Thee for Thine own sake, then withhold not from me Thine Eternal Beauty.

Rabi'a al-'Adawiyya

☪

Praise be to Thee, Most Supreme God,
Omnipotent, Omnipresent, All-pervading,
The Only Being.
Take us in Thy Parental Arms,
Raise us from the denseness of the earth.
Thy Beauty do we worship,
To Thee do we give willing surrender,
Most Merciful and Compassionate God,
The idealized Lord of the whole humanity.
Thee only do we worship, and towards Thee alone
    we aspire.
Open our hearts toward Thy Beauty,
Illuminate our souls with Divine Light,
O Thou, the Perfection of Love, Harmony, and
    Beauty!
All-powerful Creator, Sustainer, Judge, and
    Forgiver of our shortcomings,
Lord God of the East, of the West, of the worlds
    above and below,
And of the seen and unseen beings,
Pour upon us Thy Love and Thy Light,
Give sustenance to our bodies, hearts, and souls,
Use us for the purpose that Thy Wisdom chooseth,
And guide us on the Path of Thine Own Goodness.
Draw us closer to Thee every moment of our life,
Until in us be reflected Thy Grace, Thy Glory, Thy
    Wisdom, Thy Joy, and Thy Peace. Amen.

Hazrat Pir-o-Murshid Inayat Khan

Iwori Wotura,
Anybody who meets beauty and does not look at it
Will soon be poor.
The red feathers are the pride of the parrot.
The young leaves are the pride of the palm tree,
Iwori Wotura.
The straight tree is the pride of the forest.
The fast deer is the pride of the bush,
Iwori Wotura.
The rainbow is the pride of heaven.
The beautiful woman is the pride of her husband,
Iwori Wotura.
The children are the pride of the mother.
The moon and the stars are the pride of the sun,
Iwori Wotura.
Ifa says: Beauty and all sorts of good fortune arrive.

Yoruba from Nigeria

Oh you who dwell!
In the house made of the dawn,
In the house made of the evening twilight, . . .
Where the dark mist curtains the doorway,
The path to which is on the rainbow,
Where the zigzag lightning stands high on top,
Where the he-rain stands high on top,
Oh, male divinity!
With your moccasins of dark cloud, come to us.
With your leggings of dark cloud, come to us.
With your shirt of dark cloud, come to us.
With your head-dress of dark cloud, come
     to us. . . .

I have made your sacrifice.
I have prepared a smoke for you.
My feet restore for me.
My limbs restore for me.
My body restore for me.
My mind restore for me.
My voice restore for me.
Today, take away your spell from me.
Away from me you have taken it.
Far off from me you have taken it.

Happily I recover.
Happily my interior becomes cool.
Happily my eyes regain their power.
Happily my head becomes cool.
Happily my limbs regain their power.
Happily I hear again.
Happily for me the spell is taken off.
Happily I walk.
Impervious to pain, I walk.
Feeling light within, I walk. . . .

In beauty I walk.
With beauty before me, I walk.
With beauty behind me, I walk.
With beauty below me, I walk.
With beauty above me, I walk.
With beauty all around me, I walk.
It is finished in beauty,
It is finished in beauty,
It is finished in beauty.

Navaho

MERCY &
GRACE

ॐ

I salute that Madhava, the source of supreme bliss,
whose grace makes the dumb man eloquent and the
cripple cross mountains.

Bhagavad Gita

ॐ

Lord of the effulgent Universe!
It is my nature to be doing what is evil.
It is Thy nature to forbear and treat me as good.
There is now no more praise for this poor servant
    to offer Thee.
Pray deign to hasten, my Lord, to calm the mind
    of Thy poor servant; free him from sorrow and
    fear and bestow Thy Gracious Glory.
My Lord! Today is just the Time.

St. Ramalingam

ॐ

If You make me sing, I sing;
If You make me serve, I serve;
Oh my Master,
If You make me have union with You,
I have union with You;
If You torment me, I am tormented;
If You feed me any particular food,
I feed on it;
If You make me sleep, I sleep;
If, on the other hand, not allowing me to sleep,
You keep actuating me like a puppet,
Alas, what can this lowly fellow do! . . .

Whether You bestow bliss in good measure
And place me in a state of grace
Or You torment me here,
Alas, what can I do about it
Other than setting my foolish mind at rest
In the faith that Your grace alone
Is my succour?
Oh my Love, Oh my Mother,
Oh my Father Who witnesses everything,
What can be done by this lowly fellow!

St. Ramalingam

ॐ

You bestowed on me a grace undeserved by me
and enabled this slave's body and soul
to joyfully thaw and melt with love.
For this I have nothing to give in requital to You,
O Emancipator pervading the past,
the future and every thing!
O infinite primal Being! . . .

You gave Yourself to me and took me in exchange:
O Sankara,
Who, indeed, is the cleverer one of us two!
Infinite bliss I gained,
what did You gain from me?
O my Lord who has occupied my mind as Your
    shrine,
O Civan Who abides in Thirupperunthurai,
O my Father, O Lord of the Universe,
my body You have taken as Your abode;
for this I have nothing to offer in return.

Maanikkavaachakar

ॐ

I, a reprobate, am going to ruin just as I should;
O ruinless One!
You took the blame.
I shall suffer, but if I suffer all that I have to suffer,
then, what is the use of Your grace? . . .

O King! Should You not bestow grace on me?
Will it end in this wicked one being ruined?
If You will not say: "Ah! Ah!"
who is there, indeed, to tell me: "Don't fear"?
Are all those who perish without Your grace
of my standard?
Won't the devotees say
that this is undeserved in my case?
O God! O Dancer in Thillai!
I am perplexed;
will You not at least now console me?

Maanikkavaachakar

ॐ

Lord, I know You gave me this illness. I don't know what I did. Certainly, I might have done a lot, but I don't remember — maybe not in this birth, but in the past birth. So, You have given me this terrible stomach-ache.

But one thing I know, You want me to trust You completely, and probably this is the only way you can do that. You are very kind in making me think of You. The very fact that You are giving me this problem makes me happy, because with this I can never forget You. With pleasure I may forget You, but with pain, I can never forget You.

So, give me the courage; let me purge it out completely. I'm not asking You to get rid of it right away, but give me the strength, and continue to give me this problem until I purge it all out. I know You are merciful. You want to bring out the beauty, the pure part of me. So, You are simply rubbing and scrubbing me. I know that You are not unnecessarily hurting me. If there were another simpler way, You would have done it. But probably my problem is too tough; You couldn't have done it any other way.

Go ahead, do it. All I request is: give me the courage; give me the understanding; let me accept it.

Sri Swami Satchidananda
paraphrasing St. Tirunavukkarasar

ॐ

Arise! Awake! O merciful Lord!
Since long I have been calling You.
All my relations are turned enemies; I appear a
    burden to them all.
Besides You I have none whom I can call my own.
Pray pull my boat out of the stormy sea.
Beloved! without You I know no rest in the day
    and I pass my nights in wakefulness.
I stand knocking at Your door. Pray open it.
The arrow of separation has gone deep into my
    heart.
I cannot forget its pain for a moment.
Did you forget that You transformed Ahalya, who
    had been turned into stone under a curse, into a
    beautiful lady?
Then where is the occasion to neglect me who is far
    lighter than that stone statue?
So says Mirabai.

Mirabai

The Lord is gracious, and full of compassion;
Slow to anger, and of great mercy. . . .

The Lord upholdeth all that fall,
And raiseth up all those that are bowed down.

The eyes of all wait for Thee,
And Thou givest them their food in due season.

Thou openest Thy hand,
And satisfiest every living thing with favour.

The Lord is righteous in all His ways,
And gracious in all His works.

The Lord is nigh unto all them that call upon Him,
To all that call upon Him in truth.

He will fulfill the desire of them that fear Him;
He also will hear their cry, and will save them.

The Lord preserveth all them that love Him;
But all the wicked will He destroy.

My mouth shall speak the praise of the Lord;
And let all flesh bless His holy name for ever and
    ever.

from a Psalm of David

I called out of mine affliction
Unto the Lord, and He answered me;
Out of the belly of the netherworld cried I,
And Thou heardest my voice.
For Thou didst cast me into the depth,
In the heart of the seas,
And the flood was round about me;
All Thy waves and Thy billows
Passed over me.
And I said: "I am cast out
From before Thine eyes";
Yet I will look again
Toward Thy holy temple.
The waters compassed me about, even to the soul;
The deep was round about me;
The weeds were wrapped about my head.
I went down to the bottoms of the mountains;
The earth with her bars closed upon me forever;
Yet hast Thou brought up my life from the pit,
O Lord my God.
When my soul fainted within me,
I remembered the Lord;
And my prayer came in unto Thee,
Into Thy holy temple.
They that regard lying vanities
Forsake their own mercy.

But I will sacrifice unto Thee
With the voice of thanksgiving;
That which I have vowed I will pay.
Salvation is of the Lord.
And the Lord spoke unto the fish, and it
    vomited out Jonah upon the dry land.

Jonah

⛩

In each of the three wondrous worlds of life —
The past, the present, and that yet to come —
The first before our birth, the second now,
The next to open when we breathe our last —
Through all are we maintained by Grace Divine!

Tachibana-no-Sanki

⛩

The Virtue of Divine Amaterasu
Fills the Heavens and the Earth
And Her Grace has not a shadow.

Kurozumi Munetada

Everyone under heaven says that my Tao is great
and beyond compare.
Because it is great, it seems different.
If it were not different, it would have vanished
long ago.

I have three treasures which I hold and keep.
The first is mercy; the second is economy;
The third is daring not to be ahead of others.
From mercy comes courage; from economy comes
generosity;
From humility comes leadership.

Nowadays men shun mercy, but try to be brave;
They abandon economy, but try to be generous;
They do not believe in humility, but always try to be
first.
This is certain death.

Mercy brings victory in battle and strength in
defense.
It is the means by which heaven saves and guards.

Lao Tsu

Adoration to the Triple Treasure!
Adoration to Kanzeon Who is the Great
    Compassionate One!
Om to the One Who leaps beyond all fear!
Having adored Him, may I enter into the heart
    of the Noble, Adored Kanzeon!
His life is the completion of meaning; it is pure,
    it is that which makes all beings victorious and
    cleanses the path of all existence.
Om, O Thou Seer, World-transcending One!
O hail to the Great Bodhisattva!

Litany of the Great Compassionate One

Thou perfect master,
Who shinest upon all things and all men,
As gleaming moonlight plays upon a thousand
    waters at the same time!
Thy great compassion does not pass by a single
    creature.
Steadily and quietly sails the great ship of
    compassion across the sea of sorrow.
Thou art the great physician for a sick and impure
    world,
In pity giving the invitation to the "Paradise of the
    West."

from Masses for the Dead

✝

O Thou full of compassion, I commit and commend myself unto Thee, in whom I am, and live, and know. Be Thou the Goal of my pilgrimage, and my Rest by the way. Let my soul take refuge from the crowding turmoil of worldly thought beneath the shadow of Thy wings; let my heart, this sea of restless waves, find peace in Thee, O God.

St. Augustine

✝

Do not turn away, do not abandon me.
Do not leave me alone, O my Master!
You know how difficult is the route.
You know the madness of the robbers who attack us.
You know the multitude of evil wild beasts.
You know my weakness, O my Christ,
and the ignorance which I as a human being
    possess.
Besides, I do not even think I am completely
    human,
but I am much inferior to humans.
In all things, indeed, I am the last of all;
I am truly the least of all men.
Lavish me, my King and God,
with Your great mercy, I beg You,
so that this mercy would completely make up,
    O Savior,
for my deficiencies and inadequacies,
and would make of me a totally saved person,
no longer lacking the necessary things.
It would place me, Your servant, in Your presence,
O Word, as one without condemnation, without
    blame.
And I would sing Your praises, forever and ever.
Amen.

St. Symeon

In the Name of Allah, the Compassionate, the
    Merciful.

Praise be to Allah, Lord of the Creation,
The Compassionate, the Merciful,
King of the Last Judgment!
You alone we worship, and to You alone we pray
    for help.
Guide us to the straight path,
The path of those whom You have favoured,
Not of those who have incurred Your wrath,
Nor of those who have gone astray.

The Holy Koran

☪

Tell me then, who born in this world did not
    commit sin?
And how did the pious one pass his days,
    enlighten me?
If Thou takest me to task for my sin,
Where is Thy Grace, then, and tell me what is
    the difference between Thee and me? . . .

Howsoever little be Thy mercy and howsoever great
    the pangs of Thy separation,
Yet mightier and more comfortable it is than all
    the world's kindness and sympathy.
Wheresoever I loiter in this world with open eyes,
I see that where the broken heart dwells, there I find
    Thee tending the ailing one in love with Thee.

Sarmad

Never forget the Lord in your mind,
By whose kindness you get distinction in the world,
And by whose Grace you attain to Glory.
O my ignorant mind, never forget His goodness.
It is through His Grace that you fulfill your
        purposes —
Know that His presence is diffused all around you.
It is by His Grace that you realize the Truth —
O my mind, always be in harmony with Him.
I shall meditate on His Name alone,
Whose Grace it is that saves all men.

Guru Arjun

Great beyond description is His Mercy.
He, the Giver, gives all — Himself keeping nothing.
Many the warriors who seek at His door,
Countless the others who come.
Many are they who pass their lives engaged in evil.
Many are those who are granted His favor,
And enjoying themselves, they forsake their
    Creator.
Many there are who endure distress and privation,
These too are Thy blessings, O bountiful One.
It is by Thy Will that one's bonds are freed,
And he is granted liberation.
Thy ways are known only to Thee,
And if a man should dare and say he understands,
He will surely suffer by this action of his.
Our needs are known only to Him, and He alone
    fulfills.
The one whose heart He has blessed with the song
    of His praise,
Before the eyes of the world he's honored as the
    King of kings.

Guru Nanak

You, Father God,
Who are in the heavens and below,
Creator of everything and omniscient,
We are but little children
Unknowing anything evil.
If this sickness has been brought by man,
We beseech thee, help us through these roots.
In case it is inflicted by you, the Conserver,
Likewise do we entreat your mercy on your child.
Also you, our grandparents who sleep with the
    spirits of the departed,
We entreat all of you, sleep on one side.
All ancestors, males and females, great and small,
Help us in this trouble, have compassion on us,
So that we can also sleep peacefully.
And hither do I spit out this mouthful of water!
Pu-pu! Pu-pu!
Please listen to our earnest request!

Luguru from Tanzania

He, our Father,
He hath shown His mercy unto me.
In peace I walk the straight road.

Cheyenne

POWER &
STRENGTH

ॐ

Thou who art Power fill me with power.
Thou who art Valour infuse valour into me.
Thou who art Strength give me strength.
Thou who art the Vital Essence endow me with
    vitality.
Thou who art Wrath against wrong instill that wrath
    into me.
Thou who art Fortitude fill me with fortitude.

Yajur Veda

ॐ

O Force divine, supreme illuminator, listen to our prayer, do not go far from us, do not withdraw, help us to fight the good fight, fortify our strength for the struggle, give us the power for victory!

O my sweet Master, Thou whom I adore without being able to know Thee, Thou who I am without being able to realise Thee, all my conscious individuality prostrates itself before Thee and implores, in the name of the workers in their struggle, of the earth in its agony, of humanity in its suffering and of Nature in her endeavour, O my sweet Master, marvellous Unknowable, Dispenser of all boons, Thou who bringest light to birth out of darkness and force out of weakness, support our efforts, guide our steps, lead us to victory.

The Mother, Sri Aurobindo Ashram

Whilst everything around me is ever-changing, ever-dying, there is underlying all that change a Living Power that is changeless, that holds all together, that creates, dissolves, and re-creates. That informing Power or Spirit is God. . . .

In the midst of death life persists, in the midst of untruth truth persists, in the midst of darkness light persists. Hence I gather that God is Life, Truth, Light. He is Love. He is the Supreme Good. . . .

I know that I can do nothing. God can do everything. O God, make me Thy fit instrument and use me as Thou wilt.

Mahatma Gandhi

Praised be Thou, O Lord, God of our fathers, God of Abraham, Isaac, and Jacob, great, mighty, and exalted. Thou bestowest lovingkindness upon all Thy children. Thou rememberest the devotion of the fathers. In Thy love, Thou bringest redemption to their descendants for the sake of Thy name. Thou art our King and Helper, our Savior and Protector. Praised be Thou, O Lord, Shield of Abraham.

Eternal is Thy power, O Lord; Thou art mighty to save. In lovingkindness Thou sustainest the living; in the multitude of Thy mercies, Thou preservest all. Thou upholdest the falling and healest the sick; freest the captives and keepest faith with Thy children in death as in life. Who is like unto Thee, Almighty God, Author of life and death, Source of salvation? Praised be Thou, O Lord, who has implanted within us eternal life.

Thou art holy, Thy name is holy and Thy worshipers proclaim Thy holiness. Praised be Thou, O Lord, the holy God.

Sabbath prayer

Hast thou not known? hast thou not heard
That the everlasting God, the Lord,
The Creator of the ends of the earth,
Fainteth not, neither is weary?
His discernment is past searching out.
He giveth power to the faint;
And to him that hath no might He increaseth
    strength.
Even the youths shall faint and be weary,
And the young men shall utterly fall;
But they that wait for the Lord shall renew their
    strength;
They shall mount up with wings as eagles;
They shall run, and not be weary;
They shall walk, and not faint.

Isaiah

O Shang Ti— the Mightiest Emperor over all
 Heavenly Kings!
Thou, who dwellest in the Jade Hall of the
 Western Heaven,
Thou, who art remote from this poor earth and yet
 so close to us,
Thou, who enjoyest wondrous harmonies of Heaven
 and yet hearkeneth to discordant prayers of
 humble mortals,
O Almighty Spirit, Thou sitteth on the throne of
 glory and yet dost condescend to help poor
 mankind,
We pray Thee and beseech Thee to hearken to our
 humble petition.

Taoist priest

Something mysteriously formed,
Born before heaven and earth.
In the silence and the void,
Standing alone and unchanging,
Ever present and in motion.
Perhaps it is the mother of ten thousand things.
I do not know its name.
Call it Tao.
For lack of a better word, I call it great.

Being great, it flows.
It flows far away.
Having gone far, it returns.

Therefore, "Tao is great;
Heaven is great;
Earth is great;
The king is also great."
These are the four great powers of the universe,
And the king is one of them.

Man follows the earth.
Earth follows heaven.
Heaven follows the Tao.
Tao follows what is natural.

Lao Tsu

Listen to the life of Kanzeon.
To calls from every quarter He responds; . . .
When people hear His name and see His form,
And think of Him not vainly in their hearts,
All forms of ill, in all the worlds, shall cease.
If, wishing harm, an enemy should try to push
    another in a fiery pit,
The victim should on Kanzeon's great power think,
    and straightaway that fiery pit shall be trans-
    formed into a cool and silver lake. ·
If, drifting in the vast great ocean's foam, a man
    should be in danger of his life from monstrous
    fish or evil beings,
Let him only think of Kanzeon's great power, at
    once the sea will all compassion be.
If, from the top of Sumeru, a man be hurled down
    by an enemy's cruel hand,
Just let him think on Kanzeon's great power and,
    like the sun, he will remain aloft. . . .
When lightning flashes and the thunder rolls, when
    hailstones beat and rain in torrents pours,
The power of Kanzeon, if thought upon, will
    quickly clear the heavens of the storm.
If, struck by cruel disaster's hand or tortured by
    interminable pain, a being flees to Kanzeon's
    gentle arms,
He, being wise and full of mystic power, will save
    him from all worldly grief and care.

The Scripture of Kanzeon Bosatsu

✝

O God, give us, we beseech Thee, a new sense of Thy power. We are only little children. We cannot see very far. We stumble in the darkness of our ignorance and folly and sin; stumble against some law of Thy universe; catastrophe falls upon us which was beyond our power to foresee; illness takes our loved ones, death smites in a way which frightens us; the sins of others hurt and maim the purest; the whole world seems, in our moments of pessimism, in the grip of evil forces and we doubt Thy power of love.

Forgive us. Our standards are false; our values are false. The things we call power are weakness. The things we call weak are strong.

Turn our eyes to the Cross until we begin to understand the power of Love. Keep our faith pure and sweet and unspoiled by doubt even when we are wounded. Deepen our prayer life. Help us to keep our love unspoiled by bitterness. And show us Thy power until we share it; a power that nothing can quell or overcome, a love that goes on loving and never lets go in the face of all that hostility can accomplish.

So may we share in the triumph of Thy kingdom of love, when all hearts bow in willing bondage to Thee and all men join in loving service. Through Jesus Christ our Lord. Amen.

The Reverend Leslie D. Weatherhead

✝

O my God, my King! I naught can do, unless Thy Mighty Hand, unless Thy Heavenly Power, assist me.

With Thine Aid, I can do all.

St. Teresa of Avila

O God, the power is Thine, and all excellence is Thine, and it is Thou Who dost help all Thy creatures with Thy strength and Thy power, and Thou art the Doer of what Thou hast willed. Neither weakness nor ignorance are hindrances to Thee; Thou art not subject to change nor limited by past and future . . . Nothing can divert Thee from any of Thy purposes, nor is there any limit to Thy Power, nor is any place devoid of Thy Presence, nor does any affair distract Thee from any other affair.

Dhu al-Nun al-Misri

Verily Thou art able over what Thou wilt!
Thou givest the kingdom to whom Thou wilt,
    and Thou seizest the kingdom from whom Thou
    wilt;
Thou exaltest whom Thou wilt, and Thou
    abasest whom Thou wilt;
In Thy hand is the good;
Thou art powerful over all things.
Thou makest the night to enter into the day,
And Thou makest the day to enter into the night;
Thou bringest forth the living from the dead,
And Thou bringest forth the dead from the living;
And Thou providest whomsoever Thou wilt without
    reckoning.
There is no god but Thou!
Glory be to Thee, oh God, and Thine is the praise!

Supplications for the Morning

Father, O mighty force,
That force which is in everything,
Come down between us, fill us,
Until we be like Thee,
Until we be like Thee.

Susu from Guinea

O thou who rulest strength, thou Spirit of virile
    energy,
Thou canst do all, and without thee, I am
    powerless;
I who am consecrated to thee, I who am pledged
    to thee,
O Spirit, from thee I get my strength, my power.
Thou brought me the gift.
Spirit of force, I call thee. Acknowledge my call.
Come, come.
Thou must come; I gave thee what thou asked me;
The sacrifice has been given in the forest.
Spirit, I am thine, thou art mine, come to me!

Fang from Cameroon and Gabon

O Lord, your power is greater than all powers.
Under your leadership we cannot fear anything.
It is you who has given us prophetical power,
And has enabled us to foresee and interpret
    everything.
We beseech you to protect us in all trials and
    torments.
We know that you are with us,
Just as you were with our ancient ancestors.
Under your protection there is nothing that we
    cannot overcome.
Peace, praise ye Ngai,
Peace, peace, peace be with us!

Watu wa Mungu from Kenya

O Great Spirit, whose voice I hear in the winds,
and whose breath gives life to all the world,
hear me.

I come before you, one of your many children. I
am small and weak. I need your strength and
wisdom.

Let me walk in beauty and make my eyes ever
behold the red and purple sunset.

Make my hands respect the things you have made,
my ears sharp to hear your voice.

Make me wise, so that I may know the things you
have taught my people, the lesson you have
hidden in every leaf and rock.

I seek strength not to be superior to my brothers, but
to be able to fight my greatest enemy — myself.

Make me ever ready to come to you with clean
hands and straight eyes, so when life fades as a
fading sunset, my spirit may come to you
without shame.

Yellow Lark of the Sioux

O Thou kind Lord! These are Thy servants here gathered, turned towards Thy kingdom and in need of Thy blessings. O God, we are ignorant; make us wise. We are dead; make us alive. We are material; endow us with spirit. O God, resuscitate us, give us sight, give us hearing. Familiarize us with the mysteries of life, so that the secrets of Thy kingdom may become revealed to us. Thou art mighty! Thou art powerful! Thou art the Giver and Thou art the Ever-Bounteous.

'Abdu'l-Baha, Baha'i

The Force is a powerful ally. Life creates it, makes it grow. Its energy surrounds us and binds us. Luminous beings are we, not this crude matter. We must feel the Force around us, between us, everywhere.

May the Force be with us always!

Jedi prayer (adapted)

OMNIPRESENT
& FORMLESS

ॐ

O adorable Lord of mercy and love,
Salutations and prostrations unto Thee.
Thou art omnipresent, omnipotent and omniscient;
Thou art Satchidananda (Existence – Knowledge –
     Bliss Absolute);
Thou art the Indweller of all beings.
Grant us an understanding heart,
Equal vision, balanced mind,
Faith, devotion and wisdom;
Grant us inner spiritual strength to resist
     temptations
And to control the mind;
Free us from egoism, lust, greed, anger and hatred;
Fill our hearts with divine virtues.
Let us behold Thee in all these names and forms,
Let us serve Thee in all these names and forms,
Let us ever remember Thee,
Let us ever sing Thy glories,
Let Thy Name be ever on our lips,
Let us abide in Thee for ever and ever.

Sri Swami Sivananda

ॐ

In all the states of being, in all the modes of activity, in all things, in all worlds, one can meet Thee and be united with Thee, for Thou art everywhere and ever present. . . .

And that is why to find Thee is only the first step in an ascent that is infinite.

O sweet Master, sovereign Transfigurator, let all negligence and all lazy indolence cease; gather up all our energies in a sheaf and make of them a will, indomitable, irresistible.

O Light, Love, ineffable Force, all atoms cry to Thee that Thou mayest penetrate and transfigure them.

The Mother, Sri Aurobindo Ashram

ॐ

O Brahman Supreme!
Formless art thou, and yet
(Though the reason none knows)
Thou bringest forth many forms;
Thou bringest them forth, and then
Withdrawest them to thyself.
Fill us with thoughts of thee! . . .

Thou art woman, thou art man,
Thou art the youth, thou art the maiden,
Thou art the old man tottering with his staff;
Thou facest everywhere. . . .

Thou art the Primal Being.
Thou appearest as this universe
Of illusion and dream.
Thou art beyond time.
Indivisible, infinite, the Adorable One —
Let a man meditate on thee
Within his heart,
Let him consecrate himself to thee,
And thou, infinite Lord,
Wilt make thyself known to him.

Upanishads

Oh, Lord of the Universe,
I will sing Thee a song.
Where canst Thou be found,
And where canst Thou not be found?
Where I pass — there art Thou.
Where I remain — there, too, Thou art.
Thou, Thou, and only Thou.

Doth it go well — 'tis thanks to Thee.
Doth it go ill — ah, 'tis also thanks to Thee.

Thou art, Thou hast been, and Thou wilt be.
Thou didst reign, Thou reignest, and Thou wilt
    reign.

Thine is Heaven, Thine is Earth.
Thou fillest the high regions,
And Thou fillest the low regions.
Wheresoever I turn, Thou, oh Thou, art there.

Hasidic Song

Whither shall I go from Thy spirit?
Or whither shall I flee from Thy presence?
If I ascend up into heaven, Thou art there;
If I make my bed in the netherworld, behold,
    Thou art there.
If I take the wings of the morning,
And dwell in the uttermost parts of the sea;
Even there would Thy hand lead me,
And Thy right hand would hold me.
And if I say: "Surely the darkness shall envelop me,
And the light about me shall be night";
Even the darkness is not too dark for Thee,
But the night shineth as the day;
The darkness is even as the light.

from a Psalm of David

彑

There is no place
On this wide earth —
Be it the vast expanse of Ocean's waste,
Or peak of wildest mountain, sky-caressed —
In which the ever-present power divine
In every force of nature's not a shrine.

Senge-Takazumi

彑

Deem not that only in this earthly shrine
The Deity doth reign;
The earth entire, and all the Heavens Divine,
His presence do proclaim!

Shima-Shigeoyu

144

Look, it cannot be seen — it is beyond form.
Listen, it cannot be heard — it is beyond sound.
Grasp, it cannot be held — it is intangible.
These three are indefinable;
Therefore they are joined in one.

From above it is not bright;
From below it is not dark:
An unbroken thread beyond description.
It returns to nothingness.
The form of the formless.
The image of the imageless.
It is called indefinable and beyond imagination.

Stand before it and there is no beginning.
Follow it and there is no end.
Stay with the ancient Tao,
Move with the present.

Knowing the ancient beginning is the essence
    of Tao.

Lao Tsu

In all the world, in all the quarters,
There is not a place where Kanzeon does not go.
Hells, evil spirits, beastly creatures, all the evil ways
    of living, all the pain that comes from birth, old
    age, disease and death
Will, for eternity, all pass away.
Great Kanzeon views all the world in Truth,
Free from defilement, loving, knowing all,
Full of compassion;
He must always be prayed to, adored for all
    eternity.

The Scripture of Kanzeon Bosatsu

✝

Eternal power, of earth and air!
Unseen, yet seen in all around;
Remote, but dwelling everywhere;
Though silent heard in every sound; . . .

O help me God! for Thou alone
Canst my distracted soul relieve;
Forsake it not, it is Thine own,
Though weak, yet longing to believe.

Anne Brontë

O Thou, who fillest heaven and earth, ever acting,
ever at rest, who art everywhere and everywhere art
wholly present, who art not absent even when far off,
who with Thy whole being fillest yet transcendest all
things, who teachest the hearts of the faithful without
the din of words; teach us, we pray Thee.

St. Augustine

☪

What a marvel! that a Being Colourless
Displays a hundred thousand hues, shades!
What wonder! that a Being Void of Form
Enrobes in forms beyond all numbering!
May we behold Him in all hues and forms!

Thus in the name of Him who hath no name,
Yet lifts to every name an answering head,
The name of Him who is the changeless One
Amidst the changing Many, and within
Whose Oneness all this Many is confined,
May we begin our work of Peace.

Sufi writings

The Infinite is within as well as without.
Our Lord fills every heart.
He is in the earth, the sky, and the underworld;
He fills the entire universe;
He is in all vegetation, and mountains,
And our every action is according to His Will.
He fills the air, the water and the flame,
And every quarter and in ten directions,
There is no place without the Lord's Name.
It is by the Grace of that God that one
    finds peace. . . .

He it is Who is the Light of every soul;
He penetrates everywhere, up, down and around.
This faith comes to those
Who, through the Grace of the Guru, are freed from
    doubt.
The saint sees nothing but the Lord everywhere;
The law of faith governs his soul.
He hears only what is good and holy,
And he lives as one with the Omnipresent Lord.
The saints speak only of eternal Truths,
For this is the way of one who knows.
He who realizes that the One Creator is the
    Cause of every action,
Finds himself pleased with whatever comes to him.
He is within all things as well as without.
Enchanting is this vision of Him.

Guru Arjun

149

In the beginning was Kmvoum,
Today is Kmvoum,
Tomorrow will be Kmvoum.
Who can make an image of Kmvoum?
He has no body.
He is as a word which comes out of your mouth.
That word! It is no more.
It is past, and still it lives!
So is Kmvoum.

Pygmies from Zaïre

WISDOM

Heavenly Father, who graciously bestowest knowledge on man and endowest him with reason, send us the light of Thy truth, that we may gain an ever clearer insight into the wisdom of Thy ways. Banish from our hearts every desire and thought of evil, that we may truly revere Thy holy name. Forgive our sins, pardon our failings, and remove from us suffering and sorrow. May the erring and the wayward be led to know Thy lovingkindness, and to serve Thee in newness of heart; and may those who love virtue and do the right, ever be glad of Thy favor. Bless our land with plenty and our nation with peace; may righteousness dwell in our midst and virtue reign among us.

O Thou, who knowest our needs before we utter them, and ordainest all things for the best, in Thee do we forever put our trust.

Evening prayer

The world may be known
Without leaving the house;
The Way may be seen
Apart from the windows.
The further you go,
The less you will know.

Accordingly, the Wise Man
Knows without going,
Sees without seeing,
Does without doing.

Lao Tsu

O ye Knowledge-Holding Deities, pray hearken
 unto me;
Lead me on the Path, out of your great love.
When I am wandering in the Sangsara, because of
 intensified propensities,
On the bright light-path of the Simultaneously-'
 born Wisdom,
May the bands of Heroes, the Knowledge-Holders,
 lead me;
May the bands of the Mothers, the Kakinis, be my
 rear guard;
May they save me from the fearful ambuscades of
 the Bardo,
And place me in the pure Paradise Realms.

For the Transmigration

✝

O my God and my infinite Wisdom, without measure and without bounds, high above the understanding both of angels and of men! O Love, Who lovest me more than I can love myself or conceive of love! Why, Lord, have I the will to desire more than it is Thy will to give me? Why do I wish to weary myself by begging Thee for things fashioned by my desire, since Thou already knowest what are the ends of all that my understanding can conceive and my will desire, while I myself know not what is best for me? The very thing in which my soul thinks to find profit will perchance bring about my ruin. For, if I beg Thee to deliver me from a trial, the object of which is my mortification, what is it that I am begging of Thee, my God? If I beseech Thee to give it to me, perchance it may not be proportionate to my patience, which is still weak and cannot bear so great a blow; and if I suffer it with patience and am not strong in humility, I may think that I have achieved something, whereas it is Thou that art achieving it all, my God. . . .

How miserable is the wisdom of mortal man! How uncertain is his foresight! Do Thou, Who foreseest all, provide the necessary means whereby my soul may serve Thee according to Thy will and not to its own. Punish me not by giving me what I wish or desire, if Thy love (and may it ever live in me!) desire not this. May this self of mine die, and may Another, greater than myself and better for me than myself, live in me, so that I may serve Him. May He live and give me life; may He reign and may I be His captive, for my soul desires no other freedom.

St. Teresa of Avila

How rich are the depths of God — how deep his wisdom and knowledge — and how impossible to penetrate his motives or understand his methods! Who could ever know the mind of the Lord? Who could ever be his counselor? Who could ever give him anything or lend him anything? All that exists comes from him; all is by him and for him. To him be glory forever. Amen.

St. Paul

✝

Help me to be not too curious in prying into those secret things that are known only to Thee, O God, nor too rash in censuring what I do not understand. May I not perplex myself about those methods of providence that seem to me involved and intricate, but resolve them into Thine infinite wisdom, who knowest the spirits of all flesh and dost best understand how to govern those souls Thou hast created.

We are of yesterday and know nothing. But Thy boundless mind comprehends, at one view, all things, past, present, and future, and as Thou dost see all things, Thou dost best understand what is good and proper for each individual and for me, with relation to both worlds. So deal with me, O my God. Amen.

Susanna Wesley

Allah! There is no God save Him, the Alive, the Eternal. Neither slumber nor sleep overtaketh Him. Unto Him belongeth whatsoever is in the heavens and in the earth. Who is he that intercedeth with Him save by His leave? He knoweth that which is in front of them and that which is behind them, while they encompass nothing of His knowledge save what He will. His throne includeth the heavens and the earth, and He is never weary of preserving them. He is the Sublime, The Tremendous.

The Holy Koran

Guide us, O God the All-Knowing, to acquire knowledge. It enables the possessor to distinguish right from wrong; it lights the way to heaven. It is our friend in the desert, our society in solitude, our companion when friendless. It guides us to happiness; it sustains us in misery; it is an ornament among friends and armour against enemies.

Muhammad

Ho! Aged One, *eçka,*
At a time when there were gathered together seven
    persons,
You sat in the seventh place, it is said,
And of the seven You alone possessed knowledge
    of all things,
Aged One, *eçka.*

When in their longing for protection and guidance,
The people sought in their minds for a way,
They beheld you sitting with assured permanency
    and endurance
In the center where converged the paths,
There, exposed to the violence of the four winds,
    you sat,
Possessed with power to receive supplications,
Aged One, *eçka.* . . .

I have desired to go yet farther in the path of life
    with my little ones,
Without pain, without sickness,
Beyond the second, third, and fourth period of life's
    pathway,
Aged One, *eçka.*

O hear! This is my prayer,
Although uttered in words poorly put together,
Aged One, *eçka.*

Omaha

O You sacred Being of the place where the sun comes up, who controls knowledge! Yours is the path of the rising sun which brings light into the world. Your name is Huntka, for You have wisdom and are long-winged. There is a place for You in the pipe; help us in sending our voice to Wakan-Tanka! Give to us Your sacred days.

Black Elk of the Oglala Sioux

Lauded be Thy name, O my God! I testify that no thought of Thee, howsoever wondrous, can ever ascend into the heaven of Thy knowledge, and no praise of Thee, no matter how transcendent, can soar up to the atmosphere of Thy wisdom. From eternity Thou hast been removed far above the reach and the ken of the comprehension of Thy servants, and immeasurably exalted above the strivings of Thy bondslaves to express Thy mystery. What power can the shadowy creature claim to possess when face to face with Him who is the Uncreated?

Powerful art Thou to do what pleaseth Thee. Thou, truly, art the All-Glorious, the All-Wise.

Baha'u'llah, Baha'i

TRUTH

ॐ

The face of Truth is covered with a golden veil. Unveil it, O God of Light, that we who love the true may behold its glory.

Upanishads

Praised be Thy holy name. Thou hast made Thine eternal law our portion and hast given us a goodly heritage. Open our eyes to the beauty of Thy truth and help us to exemplify it in our lives that we may win all men for Thy law of righteousness. Gather all Thy children around Thy banner of truth that Thy name may be hallowed through us in all the world and the entire human family may be blessed with truth and peace. Amen.

Holiday prayer

Truth is round like the Sun
And means to be One with Amaterasu-O-Mi-Kami.

He who lives within the Truth of Heaven and Earth
Fears neither birth, nor life, nor death — nothing.

In the World nothing is so precious as Truth.
By the One Truth, all Men become Brethren.

Kurozumi Munetada

Under heaven nothing is more soft and yielding
    than water.
Yet for attacking the solid and strong, nothing is
    better;
It has no equal.
The weak can overcome the strong;
The supple can overcome the stiff.
Under heaven everyone knows this,
Yet no one puts it into practice. . . .
The truth often sounds paradoxical.

Lao Tsu

Through the Merits of Buddha, the Truth enters into us and we enter into the Truth; through the excellent power of Buddha we realise the Truth. Let us do only good for all living things that we may possess the True Mind; let us do only Pure Deeds that we may enter the peaceful world which is unchanging, Great Wisdom; let us pay homage eternally to the Buddha.

Adoration of the Buddha's Relics

Adoration to the Buddhas in the ten quarters;
Adoration to the Dharma pervading the ten
    quarters;
Adoration to the Sangha in the ten quarters; . . .
We pray that all beings will take refuge in the
    Three Treasures and share in the merit that
    fills the universe.
We pray that the light of the spirit of Truth shall
    shine of itself and pierce the darkness of
    delusion.

The Sweet Gate Scripture

✝

O Lord Jesus Christ, Thou didst not come to the
world to be served, nor to be admired, nor to be
worshipped. Thou wast the way and the truth — and
it was followers only that Thou didst demand. Arouse
us therefore if we have dozed away into this delusion;
save us from the error of wishing to admire Thee
instead of being willing to follow and resemble Thee.

Soren Kierkegaard

☪

O Allah! praise be to Thee,
Thou art the Guardian of the heavens and the earth,
And of those that are therein.
Praise be to Thee,
Thou art the light of the heavens and the earth,
And of those that are therein.
Unto Thee belongeth the praise.
Thou art the King of the heavens and the earth,
And of those that are therein.
Thou art True.
True is Thy promise.
True is our meeting with Thee.
True is Thy world.
True is heaven,
And true is hell.
True are the prophets,
True is Muhammad,
And true is the Hour of Judgment.
O Allah! unto Thee do I surrender;
In Thee I have faith;
Upon Thee do I rely;
Unto Thee do I turn.

Muhammad

Truth is His throne and Truth is His form,
And He alone dwells therein.
True are His actions and True His Word.
Yes, True is His nature which pervades all.
True are His actions and True the fruits they bear.
As true is the seed, so must be the tree.
Purest of the pure are the actions of the Lord,
And those who know Him, see good everywhere.
The True Name brings peace and joy;
True faith in the Name comes through the Guru's
    Grace.
The saints instruct us in the True Word, for they are
    true in whom God lives.
If a man were to know and be devoted to the Truth,
He would meditate on the Name and attain
    liberation.
He sees that God is True, and whatever He has
    made is also True;
God alone knows His own limits and His
    pleasure.
He who has created this world, the Creator of all
    the creation,
No one can know by any amount of contemplation.
The created cannot know the ways of the Creator;
Whatever He Wills comes to pass.

Guru Arjun

170

Thou art the great God [uTikxo] — he who is in
heaven.
It is thou, thou Shield of Truth.
It is thou, thou Tower of Truth.
It is thou, thou Bush of Truth.
It is thou, thou, who sittest in the highest.
Thou art the Creator of life, thou madest the
regions above —
The Creator who madest the heavens also,
The Maker of the stars and the Pleiades.
The shooting stars declare it unto us.

Zulu from South Africa

O Wakan-Tanka, You are the truth. The two-legged
peoples who put their mouths to this pipe will become
the truth itself; there will be in them nothing impure.
Help us to walk the sacred path of life without
difficulty, with our minds and hearts continually
fixed on You!

High Hollow Horn of the Oglala Sioux

PEACE

May there be peace in the higher regions;
May there be peace in the firmament;
May there be peace on earth.
May the waters flow peacefully;
May the herbs and plants grow peacefully;
May all the divine powers bring unto us peace.
The supreme Lord is peace.
May we all be in peace, peace, and only peace;
And may that peace come unto each of us.

The Vedas

ॐ

Like a flame that burns in silence, like a perfume that rises straight upward without wavering, my love goes to Thee; and like the child who does not reason and has no care, I trust myself to Thee that Thy Will may be done, that Thy Light may manifest, Thy Peace radiate, Thy Love cover the world. When Thou willest I shall be in Thee, Thyself, and there shall be no more any distinction; I await that blessed hour without impatience of any kind, letting myself flow irresistibly toward it as a peaceful stream flows toward the boundless ocean.

Thy Peace is in me, and in that Peace I see Thee alone present in everything, with the calm of Eternity.

The Mother, Sri Aurobindo Ashram

ॐ

O Adorable Lord! May absolute peace reign over the whole world! May wars come to an end soon! May all nations and communities be united by the bond of pure love! May all enjoy peace and prosperity! May there be deep abiding peace throughout the universe! Grant us eternal peace — the peace that passeth all understanding. May we all work together harmoniously with the spirit of self-sacrifice for the well-being of the world! May we all develop cosmic love and universal brotherhood! May we see God in all faces! May Peace be unto all!

Sri Swami Sivananda

The Lord bless thee, and keep thee;
The Lord make his face to shine upon thee, and be
    gracious unto thee;
The Lord lift up His countenance upon thee, and
    give thee peace.

Moses

When tomorrow I open my eyes
I should like to hear the news
All the children in the world
Are waiting for:
That Peace, the Redeemer, has come.

Vardit Fertouk, age 8

What shall I ask You for, God?
I have everything.
There's nothing I lack.
I ask only for one thing
And not for myself alone;
It's for many mothers, and children, and fathers —
Not just in this land, but in many lands hostile to
    each other.
I'd like to ask for Peace.
Yes, it's Peace I want,
And You, You won't deny the single wish of a girl.
You created the Land of Peace,
Where stands the City of Peace,
Where stood the Temple of Peace,
But where still there is no Peace. . . .

What shall I ask You for, God? I have everything.
Peace is what I ask for,
Only Peace.

Shlomit Grossberg, age 13

Empty yourself of everything.
Let the mind rest at peace.
The ten thousand things rise and fall while the Self
    watches their return.
They grow and flourish and then return to the
    source.
Returning to the source is stillness, which is the
    way of nature.

Lao Tsu

May creatures all abound in weal and peace;
May all be blessed with peace always;
All creatures weak or strong,
All creatures great and small,
Creatures unseen or seen,
Dwelling afar or near,
Born or awaiting birth,
— May all be blessed with peace!

Sutta-Nipata

✝

O most merciful Jesus, grant me thy grace, that it may be with me and work with me and continue with me even to the end.

Grant that I may always desire and will that which is most acceptable and pleasing in thy sight. . . .

Grant me above all things that I can desire, to desire to rest in thee and in thee to have my heart at peace.

Thou art the true peace of the heart, thou art its only rest; out of thee all things are full of trouble and difficulty. In this peace, that is, in thee, the one sovereign eternal Good, I will sleep and take my rest. Amen.

Thomas à Kempis

O Allah! You are Peace, and Peace is from You; and
Peace is really ascribed to You. Therefore, Our Lord,
let us live with Peace, and let us enter Paradise, the
House of Peace. Our Lord! You are glorified and
exalted, and You possess awe and reverence.

In Praise of Allah

O, you inhabitants of the world! Sing us the songs
    of Peace
For a life of love and friendship everlasting
So that the years of our life transpire like a pleasant
    dream
And of fear and care we know no more.

Haled Aaref abu Sherifa, age 14

Let us, O saintly friends, praise the Lord
With one-pointedness of mind and with a being that
    is ever alert.
Throughout the "Lagoon of Peace" rings the praise
    of His Name, bringing peace and harmony.
The man who gives it a place in his heart becomes
    the embodiment of all excellences,
And his every desire is fulfilled. . . .

Rare is the one whose mind realizes this treasure
    of peace,
His speech is then the praise of the Lord, his song
    the Master's Name:
That Name of which the Smritis, Vedas and
    Shastras speak.
The essence of all religions is the Name,
Which brings peace to the heart of His saints.
By the healing contact of the saints, one's sins are
    washed off;
And by their company we are released from the
    bonds of death.
But only the one whose destiny calls,
Seeks the shelter of the Lord.

Guru Arjun

O God, thou hast let me pass the night in peace,
Let me pass the day in peace.
Wherever I may go
Upon my way which thou hast made peaceable
    for me,
O God, lead my steps.
When I have spoken,
Keep off calumny from me.
When I am hungry,
Keep me from murmuring.
When I am satisfied,
Keep me from pride.
Calling upon thee, I pass the day,
O Lord who hast no Lord.

Boran from Kenya

May peace reign over the earth, may the gourd cup agree with the vessel. May their heads agree and every ill word be driven out into the wilderness, into the virgin forest.

Ewe from Dahomey, Ghana, and Togo

The clear sky,
The green fruitful earth is good;
But peace among men is better.

Omaha

ONE & UNIVERSAL

ॐ

Truth is one: sages call it by various names.
It is the one Sun who reflects in all the ponds;
It is the one water which slakes the thirst of all;
It is the one air which sustains all life;
It is the one fire which shines in all houses.
Colours of the cows may be different, but milk is
    white;
Flowers and bees may be different, but honey is
    the same;
Systems of faiths may be different, but God is one.

As the rain dropping from the sky wends its way
    towards the ocean,
So the prostrations offered in all faiths reach the
    One God, who is supreme.

Rig Veda

ॐ

May that one Para Brahman of the Hindus,
Allah of the Mohammedans,
Buddha of the Buddhists,
Ahur Mazda of the Zoroastrians,
Jehovah of the Jews,
Father in Heaven of the Christians,
The Divine Mother of the Shaktas,
Grant unto us all,
Peace, Wisdom, Prosperity, and Immortality.

Sri Swami Sivananda

Hear, O Israel: The Lord our God, The Lord is
     One.
Praised be His name whose glorious kingdom is
     forever and ever.

The Shema

The God Kuni-Tokotachi (the Earthly Eternal
    Divine Being)
Is One, and at the same time, the eight hundred
    myriads of deities.
It is the One Great Common Root of Heaven and
    Earth;
All things in the universe are in this one God.
From the beginning of the universe to its very end,
The God Kuni-Tokotachi exists everlastingly.

Izawa-Nagahide

By routes diverse men may the mountain climb,
Each path presenting different views, sublime —
But when to the proud summit they do rise,
The self-same smiling moon doth greet all eyes.

Japanese bard

From ancient times these things have arisen from
    the One:

Heaven is clear because of the One,
The earth is firm because of the One,
The Spirit is strong because of the One,
The valley is full because of the One,
The ten thousand things reproduce because of the
    One,
Leaders are able to lead because of the One.

All of this comes from the One.

If heaven were not clear it would soon split.
If the earth were not firm it would soon bend and
    break.
If the Spirit were not strong it would soon wear out.
If the valley were not full it would soon dry up.
If the ten thousand things did not reproduce they
    would soon die out.
If leaders could not lead they would soon fall.

Therefore, greatness has its source in the little.
The low is the foundation of the high.

Lao Tsu

✝

Our Father in Heaven, Creator and Sustainer of all
that lives, we seek Thy presence in a world dis-
traught, Thy love and healing in a world of enmity
and hatred. Thou hast made of one blood all the
peoples of mankind to dwell together as a family upon
the face of the earth. We come to Thee for strength to
break down the barriers that hold men apart, and to
fashion unity amidst the diversity of creed and race
and nation. Make us conscious of our common humanity. May those who are strong withhold no
opportunity from the weak, those who are powerful
keep none in subjection. Make us quick to recognize
the talents of those of other races than our own and to
give to all the honor that is their due. Forbid that we
should belie the faith we proclaim, that all men are
equal, by denying to those of other religious convic-
tions and racial ties the rights which we claim for
ourselves. Crown all our good with brotherhood. To
Thee be the honor and the glory.

And now may the search for that which is true, the
love of that which is beautiful, the enjoyment of that
which is just and good, possess our hearts and minds
as they have ennobled and enriched the lives of the
great of every age. Amen.

The Reverend Everett R. Clinchy

✝

I have a dream that one day every valley shall be exalted, every hill and mountain shall be made low, the rough places will be made plain, and the crooked places will be made straight, and the glory of the Lord shall be revealed, and all flesh shall see it together. . . .

With this faith we will be able to transform the jangling discords of our nation into a beautiful symphony of brotherhood. With this faith we will be able to work together, to pray together, to struggle together, to go to jail together, to stand up for freedom together, knowing that we will be free one day.

This will be the day when all of God's children will be able to sing with a new meaning — "My country, 'tis of thee, sweet land of liberty, of thee I sing. Land where my fathers died, land of the pilgrims' pride, from every mountainside, let freedom ring.". . .

When we let freedom ring, when we let it ring from every village and every hamlet, from every state and every city, we will be able to speed up that day when all of God's children, black men and white men, Jews and Gentiles, Protestants and Catholics, will be able to join hands and sing in the words of the old Negro spiritual: "Free at last! free at last! thank God Almighty, we are free at last!"

The Reverend Martin Luther King, Jr.

☪

Most gracious Lord, Master, Messiah, and Savior
   of Humanity,
We greet Thee with all humility.
Thou art the First Cause and the Last Effect, the
   Divine Light and the Spirit of Guidance, Alpha
   and Omega.
Thy Light is in all forms, Thy Love in all beings: in
   a loving mother, in a kind father, in an innocent
   child, in a helpful friend, in an inspiring teacher.
Allow us to recognize Thee in all Thy holy names
   and forms: as Rama, as Krishna, as Shiva, as
   Buddha.
Let us know Thee as Abraham, as Solomon, as
   Zarathustra, as Moses, as Jesus, as
   Muhammad, and in many other names and
   forms, known and unknown to the world.
We adore Thy Past; Thy Presence deeply enlightens
   our being, and we look for Thy blessing in the
   future, O Messenger, Christ, Nabi, the Rasul of
   God!
Thou whose heart constantly reaches upward, Thou
   comest on earth with a message as a dove from
   above when Dharma decays, and speakest the
   Word that is put into Thy mouth, as the light
   filleth the crescent moon.
May the Star of the Divine Light shining in Thy
   heart be reflected in the hearts of Thy devotees.

May the Message of God reach far and wide,
illuminating and making the whole Humanity
one single Brotherhood in the Fatherhood of
God. Amen.

Hazrat Pir-o-Murshid Inayat Khan

Various are the manifestations of God and various
   His ways.
Various are the guises He assumes, but He is
   ever One.
He evolves in a myriad of ways,
The One Lord, the Eternal, the Absolute.
His presence is diffused everywhere,
And he plays His many roles in an instant.
How variously He has arranged the scenes,
And only He can value the worth of His
   performance.
All hearts are His, also all places.
I live by contemplation of his Name.

Guru Arjun

O Grandfather, Father, Wakan-Tanka, we are about to fulfill Thy will as You have taught us to do in my vision. This we know will be a very sacred way of sending our voices to You; through this, may our people receive wisdom; may it help us to walk the sacred path with all the Powers of the universe! Our prayer will really be the prayer of all things, for all are really one; all this I have seen in my vision. May the four Powers of the universe help us to do this rite correctly; O Great Spirit, have mercy upon us!

Kablaya of the Oglala Sioux

Thou art one and the same God, pleased and displeased by the same things for ever.

Zoroastrianism

MAY THE ENTIRE UNIVERSE
BE EVER FILLED
WITH PEACE AND JOY,
LOVE AND LIGHT!

INDEX OF SOURCES

Derzhavin, Gavriil Romanavich (1743–1816). Outstanding Russian poet; served as Secretary of State under Catherine II: pp. 50–51.

Dhu al-Nun al-Misri (d. 860). One of the most celebrated ascetics and saints of early Sufism: p. 130.

Dinka. African people from the Sudan: pp. 14, 53.

Evening prayer. Jewish prayer for daily service: p. 153.

Ewe. African people from Dahomey, Ghana, and Togo: pp. 70, 185.

Fang. African people from Cameroon and Gabon: p. 132.

Feast of Tabernacles. Jewish harvest holiday prayer: p. 22.

Fénelon, François (1651–1715). French prelate, orator, and writer: p. 66.

Ferdusi (10th century). Persian Muslim poet: p. 52.

Fertouk, Vardit (20th century). Jewish child, eight years old when prayer was composed: p. 178.

First Prayer from Space. Given on the Apollo 8 Mission by Frank Borman, while orbiting the moon: p. 87.

For the Transmigration. Tibetan Buddhist prayer for the soul's journey after death: p. 155.

Francis of Assisi, St. (1182–1226). Founder of the Franciscan Order, which emphasizes a life of simplicity, purity, and service: pp. 47–48, 82.

Gandhi, Mahatma (1869–1948). Helped win India's freedom from British rule by means of civil disobedience; a believer in the power of Truth and in the essential unity of all faiths: pp. 13, 123.

Gobind Singh, Guru (1666–1708). Last of the ten Sikh Gurus: p. 35.

Gonara, Emperor (1496–1557). Ruler of Japan: p. 24.

Graeco-Roman. Prayer from antiquity: pp. 73–74.

Grossberg, Shlomit (20th century). Jewish child, thirteen years old when prayer was composed: p. 179.

Guaymi. Indian tribe living today in Panama and Costa Rica: pp. 37–38.

Hasidic Song. The Hasidic movement was founded in Poland in the 18th century by the Ba'al Shem Tov; a reaction to rabbinical Judaism, it taught that purity of heart is more pleasing to God than learning: p. 142.

High Hollow Horn. Holy man of the Oglala Sioux: p. 171.

Holiday prayer. Jewish prayer for the holy festivals: p. 165.

In Praise of Allah: Allah is the Islamic name for God: p. 182.

In Praise of Amitabha. Amitabha is the Buddha of Infinite Light: p. 28.

In Praise of the Virgin Mary: Christian prayer: p. 65.

Incas. Great Indian empire centered in Peru from c. 1200 to the Spanish conquest in the 16th century: p. 56.

Innuit. American or Arctic Eskimo: p. 39.

Isaiah (7th century B.C.). Major Hebrew prophet whose ministry involved criticizing the corruption in the kingdom of Judah: p. 125.

Ise Shrine. Holy Shinto shrine in Japan, where Amaterasu-O-Mi-Kami, the "Brilliant Shining Goddess," is worshiped: p. 24.

Izawa-Nagahide. Propounder of a monotheistic doctrine of Shinto: p. 191.

Japanese bard. Shinto prayer: p. 191.

Jedi prayer. Adapted from a fictional mystical religion: p. 135.

Jesus Christ (1st century). Founder of Christianity: p. 14.

John of the Cross, St. (1542–1591). Helped St. Teresa found the Reformed Order of Carmelites; known for his writings in mystical theology: p. 83.

Jonah (8th century B.C.). Hebrew prophet who was swallowed by a whale and then safely deposited on shore, so he could reform the city of Nineveh: pp. 106–107.

Kablaya. Holy man of Oglala Sioux who received the vision of the Sun Dance, an offering of the body and soul to Wakan-Tanka: pp. 38, 198.

Kempis, Thomas à (1380–1471). Augustinian monk and priest noted for writing *The Imitation of Christ*: pp. 31, 181.

Khan, Hazrat Pir-o-Murshid Inayat (1882–1927). First great Sufi master to teach in the West: pp. 93, 195–196.

Kierkegaard, Soren (1813–1855). Danish existentialist philosopher and theologian: p. 168.

Kikuyu. African people from Kenya: p. 69.

King, Martin Luther, Jr. (1929–1968). Baptist minister and leader of the civil rights movement in America: p. 194.

Konko Sect. Shinto sect founded by Konko Daijin (1813–1883): p. 63.

Koran, The Holy. The Bible of Islam: pp. 14, 33, 114, 159.

Kurozumi Munetada (1780–1850). Founded the Kurozumi Sect of Shinto, after being miraculously healed from a long illness by Amaterasu-O-Mi-Kami, the Sun-Goddess: pp. 13, 23, 44, 108, 166.

Lao Tsu (b. 604 B.C.?). Chinese sage reputed to have founded Taoism and to have written the *Tao Te Ching,* which expresses its essential teachings; there is some question as to whether he was an historic or legendary figure: pp. 13, 26–27, 45–46, 64, 109, 127, 145, 154, 166, 180, 192.

Litany of the Great Compassionate One. Buddhist prayer in praise of the great Bodhisattva Kanzeon: p. 110.

Luguru. African people from Tanzania: p. 118.

Luyia. African people from Kenya: p. 36.

Maanikkavaachakar (3rd century?). Hindu saint noted for his great work, *The Thiruvaachakam:* pp. 19, 101–102.

Masses for the Dead. Buddhist prayer: p. 111.

Mesopotamia. Ancient country in present day Iraq: p. 40.

Mexican. Prayer to Teteo-Inan, the "Mother of Gods," whose chief temple was on the spot where the Lady of Guadalupe appeared: p. 72.

Mirabai (1504–1550). Hindu saint regarded as an incarnation of divine love; renounced a royal life for one of austerity, and composed mystic songs: pp. 77, 104.

Molinos (1640–1697?). Spanish priest and mystic; founded Quietism, which taught the complete contemplative passivity of the soul before God: p. 49.

Moses (13th century B.C.). Great lawgiver of the Jewish people; led them out of bondage in Egypt to the land of Canaan: p. 178.

Mother, Sri Aurobindo Ashram (1878–1973). Born in Paris, she travelled to Pondicherry, India, to meet her guru, Sri Aurobindo, who placed her in charge of his spiritual community: pp. 79, 91, 122, 140, 176.

Moves Walking. Holy man of the Oglala Sioux: p. 55.

Muhammad (570–632). Founder of Islam; his revelations are recorded in *The Holy Koran:* pp. 85, 159, 169.

Mundaka Upanishad. Ancient Hindu scripture: p. 20. See also *Upanishads; Vedas.*

Nanak, Guru (1469–1538). Founder of the Sikh religion, which contains both Hindu and Muslim elements: p. 117.

Navaho. North American Indians having a complex religion: pp. 95–96.

Newman, Cardinal (1801–1890). English theologian and writer: p. 30.

Newton, Joseph Fort (b. 1880). Baptist minister, preacher and writer: p. 67.

Omaha. Tribe of North American Indians: pp. 14, 70, 160, 185.

Paul, St. (d. 67?). Apostle of Christ's teachings to many lands; his epistles are found in the *New Testament:* p. 157.

Psalms of David. The *Psalms* are a collection of sacred poems forming a book of the *Holy Bible.* Many were composed by David, who was king of the Hebrews from about 1013–973 B.C.: pp. 13, 21, 81, 105, 143.

Pygmies. African people from Zaïre: p. 150.

Rabi'a al-'Adawiyya (8th century). Woman Sufi saint who emphasized serving God out of love, rather than fear: pp. 85, 92.

Ramalingam, St. (1823–1874). Hindu mystic who wrote ecstatic songs in praise of God and constructed a temple in honor of God as Light; this idea has been developed in the Light Of Truth Universal Shrine (LOTUS): pp. 17, 18, 59, 99–100.

Ram Das, Guru (16th century). Fourth Sikh Guru: pp. 53, 68, 86.

Rig Veda. Ancient Hindu scripture comprising more than one thousand hymns: p. 189. See also *Vedas.*

Sabbath prayer. Jewish prayer for the holy day of rest: pp. 44, 62, 124.

Sarmad (d. 1657). Martyred poet-saint of Hindustan: p. 115.

Satchidananda, Sri Swami (b. 1914). Esteemed Yoga Master, Founder/Director of the Integral Yoga Institutes and Satchidananda Ashrams, and leader in the ecumenical movement. His vision is the inspiration for the Light Of Truth Universal Shrine (LOTUS): pp. vi–viii, ·8–10, 43, 210. *Paraphrasing St. Tirunavukkarasar:* p. 103. See also *St. Tirunavukkarasar.*

Scripture of Kanzeon Bosatsu, The. Buddhist scripture in praise of Kanzeon, the Bodhisattva of great compassion: pp. 128, 146.

Senge-Takazumi (1797–1875). High Shinto priest of the Grand Shrine of Izumo: p. 144.

Shankaracharya, Sri (686–718). One of India's greatest philosophers and teachers; reformed Hindu philosophy and founded ten monastic orders: pp. 60–61.

Shema, The. Ancient prayer expressing the central affirmation of the Jewish faith: p. 190.

Shima-Shigeoyu. Shinto priest of the Grand Shrine of Izumo during the Tokugawa Regime: p. 144.

Shinran Shonin (1173–1263). Founder of the Shin sect of Japanese Buddhism, which affirms the doctrine of salvation by faith in Amida Buddha: p. 29.

Shona. African people from Zimbabwe: p. 54.

Sivananda, Sri Swami (1887–1963). Great sage of the Himalayas who founded the Divine Life Society, which has branches throughout the world; guru of Sri Swami Satchidananda: pp. 11–12, 78, 139, 177, 190.

Sufi writings. Sufism began in the 8th century. The Sufis, Islamic mystics, emphasized divine love and union of the soul with God: p. 148.

Supplications for the Morning. Islamic prayer: p. 131.

Susu. African people from Guinea: p. 132.

Sutta-Nipata. A collection of dialogues with the Buddha, said to be among the oldest parts of the Pali Buddhist canon: pp. 64, 180.

Sweet Gate Scripture, The. Buddhist prayer: p. 167.

Symeon, St. (949–1022). Revered in Russian Orthodox Church; known as the "New Theologian": pp. 32, 113.

Tachibana-no-Sanki. Shinto theologian during the Tokugawa Regime: p. 108.

Taoist prayer (6th century): pp. 25–26.

Taoist priest. Prayer to Shang Ti, the deified emperor of the Shang dynasty, who was credited with having taught writing and agriculture to his people: p. 126.

Teresa of Avila, St. (1515–1582). Christian mystic and founder of the Reformed Order of Carmelites; famous for her writings on the interior life: pp. 84, 130, 156–157.

Tirunavukkarasar, St. (7th century). One of the four great Saivite spiritual teachers of India; also known as Appar: *paraphrased by Sri Swami Satchidananda*: p. 103.

Upanishads. The concluding portion of the Vedas, ancient Hindu scriptures. Their sublime philosophy deals with the nature of the soul, the universe, and the ultimate reality: pp. 141, 165. See also *Mundaka Upanishad; Vedas.*

Vedas, The. Ancient sacred scriptures of the Hindus, revealed by God to holy seers known as rishis. There are four collections: the *Rig, Atharva, Sama,* and *Yajur:* p. 175. See also *Mundaka Upanishad, Rig Veda, Upanishads,* and *Yajur Veda.*

Wang Wei (c. 699–761). Chinese poet, painter, and musician: p. 91.

Watu wa Mungu. An independent religious sect among the Kikuyu from Kenya: p. 133.

Weatherhead, Leslie D. (b. 1893). English minister, preacher, and writer: p. 129.

Wesley, Susanna (1669–1742). Mother of John Wesley, the founder of Methodism: p. 158.

Yajur Veda. Ancient Hindu scripture: p. 121. See also *Vedas.*

Yellow Lark. Member of the Sioux: p. 134.

Yogananda, Paramahansa (1893–1952). Indian Yoga Master who popularized Yoga in the West; founded the Self-Realization Fellowship: pp. 20, 80.

Yoruba. African people from Nigeria: p. 94.

Zend-Avesta. Zoroastrian scripture: pp. 14, 39.

Zoroastrianism. Religion founded by Zoroaster, also known as Zarathustra (c. 660–583 B.C.). A reform of the nature religion of ancient Persia, it is practiced primarily in Iran and India today: p. 198.

Zulu. People living in South Africa: p. 171.

INDEX OF
RELIGIONS

SRI SWAMI
SATCHIDANANDA

The Reverend Sri Swami Satchidananda is a much-loved and revered spiritual leader and Yoga Master. He presents the ancient teachings of Yoga in a very practical way, enabling modern seekers to benefit from their wisdom. He has dedicated his life to the cause of peace — by guiding individuals to find it within themselves and by promoting religious harmony among all people. This work has found beautiful expression in the Light Of Truth Universal Shrine (LOTUS).

Sri Swamiji is Founder/Director of the Integral Yoga Institutes and Satchidananda Ashrams, which serve as teaching and residential spiritual centers. A citizen of the world, he receives countless invitations to lecture and advise in the fields of health, education, Yoga, and ecumenism. These travels have taken him throughout the United States, Europe, Australia, and India, as well as to South America, Japan, China, and the Soviet Union. Through lectures, conferences, interviews, and books, he has inspired thousands of sincere seekers to lead lives of purity and service — dedicated to the benefit of all humanity.